MATHEMATICS
for Edexcel GCSE
STUDENT SUPPORT BOOK
(WITH ANSWERS)

Intermediate Tier

D1147114

Tony Banks and David Alcorn

Published by Causeway Press Ltd
P.O. Box 13, Ormskirk, Lancashire L39 5HP

First published 2002

© Tony Banks and David Alcorn

British Library Cataloguing-in-Publication Data.
A catalogue record for this book is available from the British Library.

ISBN 1-902796-54-3

Acknowledgements
Past exam questions, provided by *London Examinations, A Division of Edexcel*, are marked Edexcel.
The answers to all questions are entirely the responsibility of the authors/publisher and have neither been
provided nor approved by Edexcel.

Every effort has been made to locate the copyright owners of material used in this book.
Any omissions brought to the notice of the publisher are regretted and will be credited in
subsequent printings.

Page design
Billy Johnson

Reader
Anne Alcock

Artwork
David Alcorn

Cover design
Waring-Collins Partnership

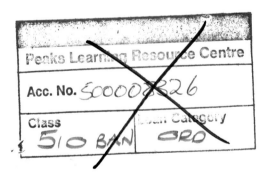

Typesetting by Billy Johnson, San Francisco, California, USA

Printed and bound by Scotprint, Haddington, Scotland

preface

This book provides detailed revision notes, worked examples and examination questions to support students in their preparation for Edexcel GCSE Mathematics at the Intermediate Tier of Entry.

The book has been designed so that it can be used in conjunction with the companion book *Mathematics for Edexcel GCSE - Intermediate Tier* or as a stand-alone revision book for self study and provides full coverage of Edexcel Specification A and Edexcel Specification B (Modular).

In preparing the text, full account has been made of the requirements for students to be able to use and apply mathematics in written examination papers and be able to solve problems in mathematics both with and without a calculator.

The detailed revision notes, worked examples and examination questions have been organised into 40 self-contained sections which meet the requirements of the National Curriculum and provide efficient coverage of the specifications.

Sections 1 - 11   Number
Sections 12 - 19   Algebra
Sections 20 - 33   Shape, Space and Measures
Sections 34 - 40   Handling Data

At the end of the sections on Number, Algebra, Shape, Space and Measures and Handling Data, section reviews are provided to give further opportunities to consolidate skills.

At the end of the book there is a final examination questions section with a further compilation of exam and exam-style questions, organised for non-calculator and calculator practice, in preparation for the exams.

contents

Number

Algebra

Shape, Space and Measures

Handling Data

Whole Numbers ●●●●●●●●●●

What you need to know

● You should be able to read and write numbers expressed in figures and words.

Eg 1 The number 8543 is written or read as, "eight thousand five hundred and forty-three".

● Be able to recognise the place value of each digit in a number.

Eg 2 In the number 5384 the digit 8 is worth 80, but in the number 4853 the digit 8 is worth 800.

● Know the Multiplication Tables up to 10×10.

● Use mental methods to carry out addition and subtraction.

● Use non-calculator methods for addition, subtraction, multiplication and division.

Eg 3 476 + 254

```
   4 7 6
 + 2 5 4
 -------
   7 3 0
   1 1
```

Eg 4 374 − 147

```
   3 ⁶7̷ ¹4
 - 1 4 7
 -------
   2 2 7
```

> **Addition and Subtraction**
> Write the numbers in columns according to place value.
> You can use addition to check your subtraction.

Eg 5 324×13

```
       3 2 4
   ×    1 3
   ----------
       9 7 2
   + 3 2 4 0
   ----------
     4 2 1 2
     1 1
```

> **Long multiplication**
> Multiply by the units figure, then the tens figure, and so on.
> Then add these answers.

Eg 6 $343 \div 7$

```
        4 9
    7) 3 4 3
       2 8
       ----
         6 3
         6 3
         ----
          0
```

> **Long division**
> ⌐→ ÷ (Obtain biggest answer possible.)
> │ Calculate the remainder.
> └─ Bring down the next figure and repeat the process until there are no more figures to be brought down.

● Know the order of operations in a calculation.

First	Brackets and Division line
Second	Divide and Multiply
Third	Addition and Subtraction

Eg 7 $4 + 2 \times 6 = 4 + 12 = 16$

Eg 8 $9 \times (7 - 2) + 3 = 9 \times 5 + 3 = 45 + 3 = 48$

Exercise 1   Do not use a calculator for this exercise.

1 Work out 769 + 236.
  (a) Give your answer in figures.   (b) Give your answer in words.

2 (a) By using each of the digits 8, 5, 2 and 3 write down
     (i)   the smallest four-digit number,   (ii) the largest four-digit number.
  (b) What is the value of the 5 in the largest number?
  (c) What is the value of the 5 in the smallest number?
  (d) What is the answer when you subtract the smallest number from the largest number?

3 The chart shows the distances in kilometres between some towns.

Tony drives from Poole to Bath and then from Bath to Selby.
  (a) How far does Tony drive?

Jean drives from Poole to Woking
and then from Woking to Selby.
  (b) Whose journey is longer?
      How much further is it?

Bath			
104	Poole		
153	133	Woking	
362	452	367	Selby

4 Work out. (a) 200×60 (b) $40\,000 \div 80$ (c) 25×7 (d) $45 \div 3$

5 Last year Mr Alderton had the following household bills.

Gas	£364	Electricity	£158	Telephone	£187
Water	£244	Insurance	£236	Council Tax	£983

He paid the bills by 12 equal monthly payments.
How much was each monthly payment?

6 A supermarket orders one thousand two hundred tins of beans.
The beans are sold in boxes of twenty-four.
How many boxes of beans are ordered?

7 Work out. (a) $6 + 4 \times 3$ (b) $96 \div (3 + 5)$ (c) $2 \times (18 - 12) \div 4$

8 Simon is 8 kg heavier than Matt. Their weights add up to 132 kg.
How heavy is Simon?

9 A roll of wire is 500 cm long. From the roll, Debra cuts 3 pieces which each measure 75 cm and 4 pieces which each measure 40 cm. How much wire is left on the roll?

10 Work out 453×73.   Edexcel

11 Car Hire Co. have the following cars available to rent.

Model	Number of cars	Weekly rental
Corsa	10	£210
Astra	12	£255
Zafira	6	£289

Work out the total weekly rental when all the cars are hired.

12 Lauren works in a car factory. She inspects 14 cars a day. Last year she inspected 3052 cars.
For how many days did she work last year?

13 Tom breeds hamsters for pet shops. The number of hamsters trebles each year.
Tom has 20 hamsters at the end of Year 1.
  (a) Copy and complete the table below.

End of year	1	2	3	4	5
Number of hamsters	20				

  (b) A hamster cage can hold no more than 14 hamsters.
      Work out the minimum number of cages needed for 900 hamsters.   Edexcel

Whole Numbers . . . Whole Numbers . . .

Decimals

What you need to know

- You should be able to use non-calculator methods for addition, subtraction, multiplication and division of decimals.

Eg 1 $2.8 + 0.56$

$$
\begin{array}{r}
2.8 \\
+\ 0.5\,6 \\
\hline
3.3\,6 \\
\hline
{\scriptstyle 1}
\end{array}
$$

Eg 2 $9.5 - 0.74$

$$
\begin{array}{r}
{}^{8}\!\not{9}.{}^{14}\!\not{5}\,{}^{1}0 \\
-\ 0.7\,4 \\
\hline
8.7\,6 \\
\hline
\end{array}
$$

> **Addition and Subtraction**
> Keep the decimal points in a vertical column.
> 9.5 can be written as 9.50.

Eg 3 0.43×5.1

$$
\begin{array}{r}
0.4\,3 \quad (2\,\text{d.p.}) \\
\times \quad 5.1 \quad (1\,\text{d.p.}) \\
\hline
4\,3 \leftarrow 43 \times 1 \\
+\ 2\,1\,5\,0 \leftarrow 43 \times 50 \\
\hline
2.1\,9\,3 \quad (3\,\text{d.p.})
\end{array}
$$

> **Multiplication**
> Ignore the decimal points and multiply the numbers.
> Count the total number of decimal places in the question.
> The answer has the same total number of decimal places.

Eg 4 $1.64 \div 0.2$

$$\frac{1.64}{0.2} = \frac{16.4}{2} = 8.2$$

> **Division**
> It is easier to divide by a whole number than by a decimal.
> So, multiply the numerator and denominator by a power of 10 (10, 100, 1000, …) to make the dividing number a whole number.

- Know how to use decimal notation for money and other measures.

- Be able to change decimals to fractions.

  Eg 5 (a) $0.2 = \frac{2}{10} = \frac{1}{5}$ (b) $0.65 = \frac{65}{100} = \frac{13}{20}$ (c) $0.07 = \frac{7}{100}$

- Carry out a variety of calculations involving decimals.

- Know that:
  when a number is **multiplied** by a number between 0 and 1 the result will be **smaller** than the original number,
  when a number is **divided** by a number between 0 and 1 the result will be **larger** than the original number.

Exercise 2

Do not use a calculator for questions 1 to 12.

1   Look at this collection of numbers.
  (a) Which number is the largest?
  (b) Which number is the smallest?
  (c) Write the numbers in ascending order.
  (d) Two of these numbers are multiplied together.
       Which two numbers will give the smallest answer?

> 13.5   0.065   0.9   4.5   23.0

2   (a) Multiply 3.2 by 100.   (b) Divide 3.2 by 100.

3 Work out. (a) $6.8 + 4.57$ (b) $4.7 - 1.8$ (c) $5 - 2.36$

4 (a) Lucy works out 0.2×0.4. She gets the answer 0.8.
Explain why her answer must be wrong.
(b) Work out (i) 0.3×0.4, (ii) 0.3×0.2.

5 Work out. (a) (i) 13.4×0.3 (ii) 4.8×2.5 (b) (i) $54.4 \div 0.4$ (ii) $0.294 \div 12$

6 Lisa has £10 to buy some stamps.
Each stamp costs 28p.
Lisa buys the greatest number of stamps she can with the £10.
(a) Work out how many stamps Lisa buys.
(b) Work out how much change she should get. *Edexcel*

7 (a) Work out $\boxed{700 \times 0.8}$ in your head.

Explain your method.

(b) Work out $\boxed{60 \div 0.4}$ in your head.

Explain your method.

8 Joseph did the following calculation: $28 \div 8.5 = 3.2$
(a) Write down the multiplication which Joseph could do to **check** his answer.
(b) Was Joseph's answer correct? Show your working. *Edexcel*

9 Using the calculation $\boxed{23 \times 32 = 736}$, work out the following.
(a) 2.3×3.2 (b) $73.6 \div 23$ (c) $736 \div 3.2$

10 Kevin is working out the time needed to complete a journey.

Using his calculator, he gets the answer $\boxed{0.66666666}$
The result is in hours.
How many minutes will the journey take?

11 $5 \times m$ gives an answer **less than 5**.
$5 \div m$ gives an answer **more than 5**.
Give two possible values for m which satisfy **both** conditions.

12 Two pieces of wood of length $0.75\,\text{m}$ and $2.68\,\text{m}$ are sawn from a plank $5\,\text{m}$ long.
What length of wood is left?

13 Potatoes are sold in bags and sacks.
Bags of potatoes weigh $2.5\,\text{kg}$ and cost 95 pence.
Sacks of potatoes weigh $12\,\text{kg}$ and cost £3.18.
How much, per kilogram, is saved by buying sacks of potatoes instead of bags of potatoes?

14 Apples cost 99p per kilogram.
Work out the total cost of $3.65\,\text{kg}$ of apples. *Edexcel*

15 The distance by road from Maidstone to Manchester is approximately 250 miles.
Work out an estimate for this distance in kilometres, given that 1 kilometre is about 0.62 miles. *Edexcel*

16 Work out $\dfrac{12.9 \times 7.3}{3.9 + 1.4}$. Write down your full calculator display.

17 Use your calculator to work out the exact value of $\dfrac{14.82 \times (17.4 - 9.25)}{(54.3 + 23.7) \times 3.8}$ *Edexcel*

Approximation and Estimation

What you need to know

● How to **round** to the nearest 10, 100, 1000.

Eg 1 Write 6473 to   (a) the nearest 10,   (b) the nearest 100,   (c) the nearest 1000.
                    (a) 6470   (b) 6500   (c) 6000

● How to approximate using **decimal places**.

Write the number using one more decimal place than asked for.
Look at the last decimal place and
  ● if the figure is 5 or more round up,
  ● if the figure is less than 5 round down.

Eg 2 Write the number 3.649 to
  (a) 2 decimal places,
  (b) 1 decimal place.

  (a) 3.65
  (b) 3.6

● How to approximate using **significant figures**.

Start from the most significant figure and count the required number of figures.
Look at the next figure to the right of this and
  ● if the figure is 5 or more round up,
  ● if the figure is less than 5 round down.
Add noughts, as necessary, to locate the decimal point and preserve the place value.

Eg 3 Write each of these numbers correct to 2 significant figures.
  (a) 365
  (b) 0.0423

  (a) 370
  (b) 0.042

● You should be able to choose a suitable degree of accuracy.

The result of a calculation involving measurement should not be given to a greater degree of accuracy than the measurements used in the calculation.

● Be able to use approximations to estimate that the actual answer to a calculation is of the right order of magnitude.

Eg 4 Use approximations to estimate $\dfrac{5.1 \times 57.2}{9.8}$

$$\dfrac{5 \times 60}{10} = 30$$

Estimation is done by approximating every number in the calculation to one significant figure.
The calculation is then done using the approximated values.

Exercise 3

Do not use a calculator for questions 1 to 12.

1 Write the result shown on the calculator display
  (a) to the nearest whole number,
  (b) to the nearest ten,
  (c) to the nearest hundred.

626.47

2 A newspaper's headline states: "20 000 people attend concert".
The number in the newspaper is given to the nearest thousand.
What is the smallest possible attendance?

3 The diagram shows the distances between towns A, B and C.

A ←————— 287 km —————→ B ←— 114 km —→ C

By rounding each of the distances given to the nearest hundred, estimate the distance between A and C.

4 On Saturday a dairy sold 2975 litres of milk at 42 pence per litre.
By rounding each number to one significant figure, estimate the amount of money received from the sale of milk, giving your answer in pounds.

5 (a) Write down two numbers you could use to get an approximate answer to 41×89.
(b) Work out your approximate answer.
(c) Work out the difference between your approximate answer and the exact answer.   Edexcel

6 Find an estimate for $2019 \div 37$, showing your working clearly.

7 (a) To estimate 97×49 Charlie uses the approximations 100×50.
Explain why his estimate will be larger than the actual answer.
(b) To estimate $1067 \div 48$ Patsy uses the approximations $1000 \div 50$.
Will her estimate be larger or smaller than the actual answer?
Give a reason for your answer.

8 A concert hall has 22 rows of seats. Each row has 69 seats.
(a) Work out an approximate answer to the total number of seats in the concert hall.

Every person attending a concert pays £9.75 on entry. Every seat in the concert hall is filled.
(b) Work out the approximate amount of money taken at the concert hall.   Edexcel

9 Clint has to calculate $\dfrac{414 + 198}{36}$

He calculates the answer to be 419.5.
By rounding each number to one significant figure estimate whether his answer is about right. Show all your working.

10 Explain how you can **estimate** the value of the following by approximating the three numbers and give your approximate answer. $\dfrac{0.251 \times 81.376}{5.096}$ Edexcel

11 In 2001 Mr Symms drove 8873 kilometres.
His car does 11 kilometres per litre. Petrol costs 69.9 pence per litre.
Use approximations to estimate the amount he spent on petrol.

12 Melanie needs 200 crackers for an office party.
The crackers are sold in boxes of 12.
How many boxes must she buy?

13 Calculate $97.2 \div 6.5$.
Give your answer correct to   (a) two decimal places,   (b) one decimal place.

14 Calculate 78.4×8.7.
Give your answer correct to   (a) two significant figures,   (b) one significant figure.

15 (a) Calculate $\dfrac{88.3 \times 4.24}{72.5 - 9.87}$.

(b) By using approximations show that your answer to (a) is about right.
You **must** show all your working.   Edexcel

Negative Numbers

What you need to know

- You should be able to use **negative numbers** in context, such as temperature, bank accounts.
- Realise where negative numbers come on a **number line**.

- Be able to put numbers in order (including negative numbers).

  Eg 1 Write the numbers $19, -3, 7, -5$ and 0 in ascending order.
  $$-5, \quad -3, \quad 0, \quad 7, \quad 19$$

- Add $(+)$, subtract $(-)$, multiply $(\times)$ and divide $(\div)$ with negative numbers.
  To **add** or **subtract** negative numbers: Use these rules to **multiply** or **divide**
  Replace double signs with a single sign.   negative numbers.

| $+ \; +$ can be replaced by $+$ |
| $- \; -$ can be replaced by $+$ |
| $+ \; -$ can be replaced by $-$ |
| $- \; +$ can be replaced by $-$ |

When multiplying:	When dividing:
$+ \times + = +$	$+ \div + = +$
$- \times - = +$	$- \div - = +$
$+ \times - = -$	$+ \div - = -$
$- \times + = -$	$- \div + = -$

  Eg 2 Work out.

  (a) $(-3) + (-2)$ (b) $(-5) - (-8)$ (c) $(-2) \times (-3)$ (d) $(-8) \div (+2)$
  $\quad\;\; = -3 - 2$ $\quad\;\; = -5 + 8$ $\quad\;\; = 6$ $\quad\;\; = -4$
  $\quad\;\; = -5$ $\quad\;\; = 3$

Exercise 4

Do not use a calculator for this exercise.

1 What temperatures are shown by these thermometers?

(a)   (b)

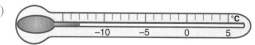

2 The midday temperatures in three different places on the same day are shown.

| Moscow $-7°C$ Oslo $-9°C$ Warsaw $-5°C$ |

(a) (i)   Which place was coldest?   (ii)   Which place was warmest?
(b)   The temperature in Siberia is $17°C$ less than the temperature in Moscow.
    What is the temperature in Siberia?

3 Place the following numbers in order of size, starting with the smallest.

$$17 \quad -9 \quad -3 \quad 5 \quad 0 \quad 7$$

4 Work out.   (a) $-5 + 10$ (b) $-5 - 10$ (c) $-5 - (-10)$

5 What number must be placed in the box to complete each of the following?
(a) $-4 + \square = 2$ (b) $-2 - \square = -1$

6 The top of a cliff is 125 m above sea level.
The bottom of the lake is 15 m below sea level.
How far is the bottom of the lake below the
top of the cliff?

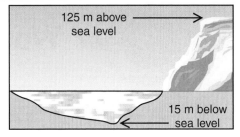

125 m above
sea level

15 m below
sea level

7 The table shows the maximum and minimum temperatures for five cities during one year.

City	Maximum	Minimum
Chicago	30°C	−15°C
Bombay	37°C	12°C
London	34°C	−12°C
Montreal	26°C	−17°C
Reykjavik	17°C	−14°C

(a) Which city had the lowest temperature?
(b) Work out the difference between the maximum temperature and the minimum temperature
for Chicago.   Edexcel

8 Gordon has £28 in his bank account.
He pays a bill of £85 by cheque, which is accepted by his bank.
What is the new balance in his account?

9 The table shows the temperatures recorded at a ski resort one day in February.

Time	0600	1200	1800	2400
Temperature (°C)	−3	3	−2	−6

(a) By how many degrees did the temperature rise between 0600 and 1200?
(b) During which six-hourly period was the maximum drop in temperature recorded?

10 The ice cream is stored at −25°C.
How many degrees is this below the
required storage temperature?

ICE CREAM
Store below
−18°C

11 Find the value of   (a) $-7 - (-3)$,   (b) -2×4.   Edexcel

12 Work out.   (a) (i) $(+5) \times (-4)$ (ii) $(-7) \times (-3)$
               (b) (i) $(-12) \div (+3)$ (ii) $(-15) \div (-5)$

13 This rule can be used to estimate the temperature in °F for temperatures given in °C.

> Multiply the temperature in °C by 2 and add 30.

Use this rule to estimate -5°C in °F.

14 Work out.   (a) $\dfrac{(-2) \times (-5) \times (+6)}{(-3)}$ (b) $(-3) + (-2) \times (+6)$

15 A test has 12 questions.

> A correct answer scores $+3$ marks.
> An incorrect answer scores -1 mark.

Pippa attempts every question and scores 8 marks.
How many correct answers did she get?

- **Multiples** of a number are found by multiplying the number by   1,   2,   3,   4,   …

  Eg 1   The multiples of 8 are $1 \times 8 = \mathbf{8}$, $2 \times 8 = \mathbf{16}$, $3 \times 8 = \mathbf{24}$, $4 \times 8 = \mathbf{32}$,   …

- You can find **all** the **factors** of a number by finding all the multiplication facts that give the number.

  Eg 2 $1 \times 6 = 6$ and $2 \times 3 = 6$.   So, the factors of 6 are: 1,   2,   3   and   6.

- A **prime number** is a number with only two factors, 1 and the number itself.
  The first few prime numbers are: 2,   3,   5,   7,   11,   13,   17,   19,   …
  The number 1 is not a prime number because it has only one factor.

- The **prime factors** of a number are those factors of the number which are themselves prime numbers.

  Eg 3   The factors of 18 are: 1,   2,   3,   6,   9   and   18.
  The prime factors of 18 are: 2   and   3.

- The **Least Common Multiple** of two numbers is the smallest number that is a multiple of them both.

  Eg 4   The Least Common Multiple of 4 and 5 is 20.

- The **Highest Common Factor** of two numbers is the largest number that is a factor of them both.

  Eg 5   The Highest Common Factor of 8 and 12 is 4.

- An expression such as $3 \times 3 \times 3 \times 3 \times 3$ can be written in a shorthand way as 3^5.
  This is read as '3 to the power of 5'. The number 3 is the **base** of the expression. 5 is the **power**.

- Powers can be used to help write any number as the **product of its prime factors**.

  Eg 6 $72 = 2 \times 2 \times 2 \times 3 \times 3 = 2^3 \times 3^2$

- Numbers raised to the power of 2 are **squared**.

  Squares can be calculated using the $\boxed{x^2}$ button on a calculator.

  The opposite of squaring a number is called finding the **square root**.
  Square roots can be calculated using the $\boxed{\sqrt{}}$ button on a calculator.

  The square root of a number can be positive or negative.

Square numbers are whole numbers squared. The first few square numbers are: 1, 4, 9, 16, 25, 36, …

  Eg 7   The square root of 9 is $+3$ or -3.

- Numbers raised to the power of 3 are **cubed**.
  The opposite of cubing a number is called finding the **cube root**.

  Cube roots can be calculated using the $\boxed{\sqrt[3]{}}$ button on a calculator.

Cube numbers are whole numbers cubed. The first few cube numbers are: 1, 8, 27, 64, 125, …

- **Powers**
  The squares and cubes of numbers can be worked out on a calculator by using the $\boxed{x^y}$ button.
  The $\boxed{x^y}$ button can be used to calculate the value of a number x raised to the power of y.

  Eg 8 Calculate 2.6^4.
  Enter the sequence: $\boxed{2}$ $\boxed{.}$ $\boxed{6}$ $\boxed{x^y}$ $\boxed{4}$ $\boxed{=}$. So $2.6^4 = 45.6976$

- The **reciprocal** of a number is the value obtained when the number is divided into 1.

  Eg 9 The reciprocal of 2 is $\frac{1}{2}$.

  The reciprocal of a number can be found on a calculator by using the $\boxed{\frac{1}{x}}$ button.

  > A number times its reciprocal equals 1.
  > Zero has no reciprocal.
  > The reciprocal of a number can be shown using an index of -1.

  Eg 10 Find the reciprocal of 5.
  The reciprocal of $5 = 5^{-1} = \frac{1}{5} = 0.2$
  Using a calculator, press: $\boxed{5}$ $\boxed{\frac{1}{x}}$

- Square roots and cube roots can be found using a method called **trial and improvement**.

  > When using trial and improvement:
  > Work methodically using trials first to the nearest whole number, then to one decimal place etc.
  > Do at least one trial to one more decimal place than the required accuracy to be sure of your answer.

- Powers of the same base are **added** when terms are **multiplied**.
  Powers of the same base are **subtracted** when terms are **divided**.

  Eg 11 (a) $2^3 \times 2^2 = 2^5$ (b) $2^3 \div 2^2 = 2^1 = 2$

  > In general: $a^m \times a^n = a^{m+n}$
  > $a^m \div a^n = a^{m-n}$
  > $a^1 = a$
  > $a^0 = 1$

- Any number raised to the power zero equals 1.

- A surd is the square root of a positive integer, like $\sqrt{3}$, for which the root is not exact.

  > $\sqrt{9}$ is not a surd because it has an exact root.
  > To keep an exact answer it is therefore necessary to keep numbers like $\sqrt{3}$ in surd form.

- You should be able to use a calculator to solve a variety of problems.

Exercise 5   Do not use a calculator for questions 1 to 17.

1 (a) Write down all the factors of 18.
   (b) Write down a multiple of 7 between 30 and 40.
   (c) Explain why 15 is not a prime number.

2 Look at these numbers. | 2 | 5 | 8 | 11 | 14 | 17 | 20 |

   (a) Which of these numbers are factors of 10?
   (b) Which of these numbers is a multiple of 10?
   (c) Which of these numbers are prime numbers?

3 (a) What is the square of 6?
   (b) What is the square root of 100?
   (c) What is the cube of 3?
   (d) What is the cube root of 8?

4 A number of counters can be grouped into 2's, 3's, 4's and 5's.
   Find the smallest possible number of counters.

5 Write down the value of (a) $\sqrt{25}$, (b) the cube of 4.

Edexcel

6 Look at these numbers. | 2 | 15 | 27 | 36 | 44 | 51 | 64 |
(a) Which of these numbers is a prime number?
(b) Which of these numbers is both a square number and a cube number?

7 Find the value of (a) $\sqrt{9} + \sqrt{16}$, (b) $\sqrt{121} \times 4^2$.

8 Find the value of $\sqrt{(2 \times 2 \times 3 \times 3 \times 5 \times 5)}$

Edexcel

9 (a) Write 36 as a product of its prime factors.
(b) Write 45 as a product of its prime factors.
(c) What is the highest common factor of 36 and 45?
(d) What is the least common multiple of 36 and 45?

10 A white light flashes every 10 seconds. A red light flashes every 6 seconds.
The two lights flash at the same time.
After how many seconds will the lights next flash at the same time?

11 (a) What is the cube root of 125?
(b) What is the reciprocal of 4?

12 Work out. (a) $2^3 \times 3^2$ (b) $\left(\sqrt{9} \times \sqrt{25}\right)^2$ (c) $2^3 \times \sqrt[3]{64}$

13 (a) Which is smaller $\sqrt{225}$ or 2^4? Show your working.
(b) Work out the value of $3^1 - 3^0$.

14 Find the value of x in each of the following.
(a) $7^6 \times 7^3 = 7^x$ (b) $7^6 \div 7^3 = 7^x$ (c) $(7^6)^3 = 7^x$ (d) $7^0 = x$

15 Simplify fully each of these expressions. Leave your answers in power form.
(a) $3^2 \times 3^3$ (b) $4^{-2} \times 4^5$ (c) $5^6 \div 5^3$ (d) $9^4 \div 9^{-2}$ (e) $\dfrac{2^3 \times 2}{2^6}$

16 Which is bigger 2^3 or the reciprocal of 0.1? Show your working.

17 (a) Between which two consecutive whole numbers does $\sqrt{70}$ lie?
(b) Use a trial and improvement method to find the square root of 70 correct to two decimal places. Show your working clearly.

18 Find the reciprocal of 7.
Give your answer correct to two decimal places.

19 (a) Use your calculator to find the value of $5.43 \times \sqrt{(18 - 6.67)}$.
Write down all the figures on your calculator display.
(b) Give your answer to part (a) correct to 2 decimal places.

Edexcel

20 Use your calculator to find the value of $\sqrt{47.3^2 - 9.1^2)}$.
(a) Write down all the figures on your calculator display.
(b) Write your answer to part (a) correct to 2 significant figures.

Edexcel

21 Use your calculator to work out the value of $\dfrac{\sqrt{12.3^2 + 7.9}}{1.8 \times 0.17}$
Give your answer correct to 1 decimal place.

Edexcel

22 (a) Calculate the value of $\sqrt{\dfrac{4.1}{(0.19)^2}}$.

(b) Show how to check that your answer is of the right order of magnitude.

Standard Index Form

What you need to know

- **Standard index form**, or **standard form**, is a shorthand way of writing very large and very small numbers.

- In **standard form** a number is written as: **a number between 1 and 10 × a power of 10**
  Large numbers (ten, or more) have a **positive** power of 10.

  Eg 1 Write 370 000 in standard form.
  $370\ 000 = 3.7 \times 100\ 000 = 3.7 \times 10^5$

  Eg 2 Write 5.6×10^7 as an ordinary number.
  $5.6 \times 10^7 = 5.6 \times 10\ 000\ 000 = 56\ 000\ 000$

  Small positive numbers (less than one) have a **negative** power of 10.

  Eg 3 Write 0.000 73 in standard form.
  $0.000\ 73 = 7.3 \times 0.000\ 1 = 7.3 \times 10^{-4}$

  Eg 4 Write 2.9×10^{-6} as an ordinary number.
  $2.9 \times 10^{-6} = 2.9 \times 0.000\ 001 = 0.000\ 002\ 9$

- You should be able to interpret the display on a calculator.

  Eg 5 The calculator display shows the answer to 0.007×0.09
  In standard form, the answer is 6.3×10^{-4}
  As an ordinary number, the answer is 0.000 63

6.3   −04

- You should be able to solve problems involving numbers given in standard form.

Exercise 6

Do not use a calculator for questions 1 to 7.

1 Write one million in standard form.

2 Look at these numbers.

2.6×10^4	6.2×10^3	9.8×10^{-4}	8.9×10^{-5}

(a) (i) Which number is the largest? (ii) Write your answer as an ordinary number.
(b) (i) Which number is the smallest? (ii) Write your answer as an ordinary number.

3 (a) Write 57 000 000 in standard index form.
(b) Write 0.000 057 in standard index form.

4 Work out.
(a) $(6 \times 10^3) + (5 \times 10^4)$ (b) $(6 \times 10^3) \times (5 \times 10^4)$ (c) $(6 \times 10^3) \div (5 \times 10^4)$
Give your answers in standard form.

5 Work out $4 \times 10^8 - 4 \times 10^6$.
Give your answer in standard form. Edexcel

6 The mass of an atom of oxygen is 0.000 000 000 000 000 000 000 027 grams.
(a) Write this number in standard form.
(b) Calculate, in standard form, the mass of 5×10^8 atoms of oxygen Edexcel

7 The table shows the populations of four countries in Latin America.

Country	Population
Belize	2.0×10^5
Guatemala	1.2×10^7
Mexico	1.1×10^8
Nicaragua	4.9×10^6

(a) Which of these countries has the largest population?
(b) How many more people live in Nicaragua than in Belize?
(c) What is the total population of these four countries?
Give your answer in standard form.

8 (a) Write 0.000 006 in standard form.

(b) Work out $\dfrac{3 \times 10^4}{5 \times 10^{-5}}$, giving your answer in standard form.

9 The mass of a neutron is 1.675×10^{-24} grams.
Calculate the total mass of 1500 neutrons.
Give your answer in standard form.

Edexcel

10 Last Sunday 1.85 million copies of a newspaper were printed.
Each of these newspapers weighed 234 grams.
Calculate the total weight of these newspapers in kilograms.
Give your answer in standard form.

11 (a) Calculate $\dfrac{7.2 \times 10^6}{0.0045}$.

Give your answer in standard form.

(b) Calculate $\dfrac{530}{6.7 \times 10^5}$.

Give your answer as an ordinary number correct to two significant figures.

12 In Astronomy, the distance between stars is measured in light years.
A light year is approximately 9.46×10^{12} kilometres.
Alpha Cygni is approximately 1.05×10^{14} kilometres from the Sun.
How many light years is Alpha Cygni from the Sun?

13 The volume of Elspeth's house is 379.6m³.
(a) Write 379.6 in standard form.

The heat, H, needed to keep a house warm is given by the formula

$$H = \frac{5544 \times 1.4 \times 3 \times 22.5 \times \text{Volume of house}}{2000}$$

(b) Calculate the value of H for Elspeth's house, giving your answer in standard form.

Edexcel

14 Work out $\dfrac{3.5 \times 10^{-3}}{4.1 \times 10^2}$.

Give your answer as an ordinary number correct to 2 significant figures.

15 Work out $\dfrac{(3.5 \times 10^6) \times (5 \times 10^{-4})}{2.5 \times 10^5}$.

Give your answer as an ordinary number.

Fractions

What you need to know

- The top number of a fraction is called the **numerator**, the bottom number is called the **denominator**.

- Fractions which are equal are called **equivalent fractions**.

  | **To write an equivalent fraction:**
  Multiply the numerator and denominator by the **same** number.

  Eg 1 $\frac{1}{4} = \frac{1 \times 3}{4 \times 3} = \frac{1 \times 5}{4 \times 5}$

  $\frac{1}{4} = \frac{3}{12} = \frac{5}{20}$

- In its **simplest form**, the numerator and denominator of a fraction have no common factor, other than 1.

- $2\frac{1}{2}$ is an example of a **mixed number**. It is a mixture of whole numbers and fractions.

- $\frac{5}{2}$ is an **improper** (or '**top heavy**') fraction.

- Fractions must have the **same denominator** before **adding** or **subtracting**.

  Eg 2 Work out.

  (a) $\frac{3}{4} + \frac{2}{3} = \frac{9}{12} + \frac{8}{12} = \frac{17}{12} = 1\frac{5}{12}$

  (b) $\frac{4}{5} - \frac{1}{2} = \frac{8}{10} - \frac{5}{10} = \frac{3}{10}$

  | Add (or subtract) the numerators only. When the answer is an improper fraction change it into a mixed number.

- Mixed numbers must be changed to **improper fractions** before **multiplying** or **dividing**.

  Eg 3 Work out.

  (a) $1\frac{1}{4} \times 2\frac{1}{5} = \frac{5}{4} \times \frac{11}{5} = \frac{11}{4} = 2\frac{3}{4}$

  (b) $1\frac{1}{3} \div 1\frac{3}{5} = \frac{4}{3} \div \frac{8}{5} = \frac{4}{3} \times \frac{5}{8} = \frac{5}{6}$

  | The working can be simplified by dividing a numerator and a denominator by the same number.

  | Notice that dividing by $\frac{8}{5}$ is the same as multiplying by $\frac{5}{8}$.

- All fractions can be written as decimals.

  | To change a fraction to a decimal divide the **numerator** by the **denominator**.

  Eg 4 Change $\frac{4}{5}$ to a decimal.

  $\frac{4}{5} = 4 \div 5 = 0.8$

- Some decimals have **recurring digits**. These are shown by:

  a single dot above a single recurring digit,

  Eg 5 $\frac{2}{3} = 0.6666\ldots = 0.\dot{6}$

  a dot above the first and last digit of a set of recurring digits. **Eg 6** $\frac{5}{11} = 0.454545\ldots = 0.\dot{4}\dot{5}$

Exercise 7

Do not use a calculator for this exercise.

1 Each of these pairs of fractions are equivalent. In each case find the value of n.

(a) $\frac{3}{5}$ and $\frac{n}{15}$ (b) $\frac{n}{3}$ and $\frac{8}{12}$ (c) $\frac{6}{8}$ and $\frac{15}{n}$

2 (a) Which of the fractions $\frac{7}{10}$ or $\frac{4}{5}$ is the smaller? Explain why.

(b) Write down a fraction that lies halfway between $\frac{1}{3}$ and $\frac{1}{2}$.

3 Write these fractions in order of size, with the smallest first. $\frac{2}{5}$ $\frac{3}{8}$ $\frac{1}{4}$ $\frac{7}{20}$

4 Work out $\frac{3}{8}$ of £32.

5 This rule can be used to change kilometres into miles.

> Multiply the number of kilometres by $\frac{5}{8}$

Flik cycles 24 kilometres. How many miles is this?

6 Jan uses $\frac{3}{4}$ of a jar of cherries to make a cheesecake.
How many jars of cherries does she need to buy to make 10 cheesecakes?

7 An examination is marked out of 48.
Ashley scored 32 marks.
What fraction of the total did he score?
Give your answer in its simplest form.

8 Ann wins £160. She gives $\frac{1}{4}$ of £160 to Pat, $\frac{3}{8}$ of £160 to John and £28 to Peter.
What fraction of the £160 does Ann keep? Give your fraction in its simplest form. Edexcel

9 The cake stall at a school fete has 200 fairy cakes for sale.
It sells $\frac{3}{5}$ of them at 25p each and the remainder at 20p each.
How much money does the stall get from selling fairy cakes?

10 George pays £1.82 for $\frac{1}{5}$ kg of toffees at £4.20 per kilogram and $\frac{1}{4}$ kg of jellies.
How much per kilogram are jellies?

11 Work out. (a) $\frac{3}{5} \times \frac{1}{2}$ (b) $\frac{3}{4} - \frac{1}{3}$ (c) $1\frac{1}{2} + 2\frac{3}{5}$

12 (a) Change $\frac{1}{6}$ to a decimal. Give the answer correct to 3 d.p.

(b) Write these numbers in order of size, starting with the largest.

> 1.067   1.7   1.66 $1\frac{1}{6}$ 1.67

13 Income tax and national insurance take $\frac{1}{5}$ of Phillip's pay.
He gives $\frac{2}{5}$ of what he has left to his parents for housekeeping.
What fraction of his pay does Phillip have left for himself?

14 Three-fifths of the people at a party are boys. Three-quarters of the boys are wearing fancy dress.
What fraction of the people at the party are boys wearing fancy dress?

15 Edward, Marc, Dee and Lin share an apple pie. Edward has $\frac{1}{3}$, Marc has $\frac{1}{5}$ and Dee has $\frac{1}{4}$.
What fraction of the pie is left for Lin?

16 Work out. (a) $4 - 1\frac{2}{3}$ (b) $\frac{3}{4} \times 1\frac{1}{5}$ (c) $4\frac{1}{2} \div \frac{3}{8}$

17 Which of the following fractions is nearest to $\frac{3}{4}$? $\quad \frac{7}{10} \qquad \frac{2}{3} \qquad \frac{7}{8} \qquad \frac{9}{11}$
Show how you decide.

18 In a sale the price of a microwave is reduced by $\frac{1}{5}$.
The sale price is £96.
What was the price of the microwave before the sale?

Percentages

What you need to know

- 10% is read as '10 percent'. 'Per cent' means out of 100. 10% means 10 out of 100.

- A percentage can be written as a fraction, 10% can be written as $\frac{10}{100}$.

- To change a decimal or a fraction to a percentage: **multiply by 100**.

  Eg 1 Write as a percentage (a) 0.12   (b) $\frac{8}{25}$

  (a) $0.12 \times 100 = 12\%$ (b) $\frac{8}{25} \times 100 = 32\%$

- To change a percentage to a fraction or a decimal: **divide by 100**.

  Eg 2 Write 18% as (a) a decimal,   (b) a fraction.

  (a) $18\% = 18 \div 100 = 0.18$ (b) $18\% = \frac{18}{100} = \frac{9}{50}$

- How to express one quantity as a percentage of another.

  Eg 3 Write 30p as a percentage of £2.

  $\frac{30}{200} \times 100 = 30 \times 100 \div 200 = 15\%$

  > Write the numbers as a fraction, using the same units.
  > Change the fraction to a percentage.

- You should be able to use percentages to solve a variety of problems.

- Be able to find a percentage of a quantity.

  Eg 4 Find 20% of £64.
  £64 ÷ 100 = £0.64
  £0.64 × 20 = £12.80

  > 1. Divide by 100 to find 1%.
  > 2. Multiply by the percentage to be found.

- Be able to find a percentage increase (or decrease).

  Eg 5 Find the percentage loss on a micro-scooter bought for £25 and sold for £18.

  Percentage loss = $\frac{7}{25} \times 100 = 28\%$

  > Percentage decrease = $\frac{\text{actual decrease}}{\text{initial value}} \times 100\%$
  >
  > Percentage increase = $\frac{\text{actual increase}}{\text{initial value}} \times 100\%$

- Be able to solve reverse percentage problems.

  Eg 6 Find the original price of a car which is sold at a loss of 20% for £1200.

  80% of original price = £1200
  1% of original price = £1200 ÷ 80 = £15
  Original price = £15 × 100 = £1500

  > First find 1% of the original value by dividing the selling price by (100 − % loss), then multiply by 100.

Exercise 8

Do not use a calculator for questions 1 to 7.

1 Write 0.4, $\frac{9}{20}$ and 42% in order of size, smallest first.

2 Work out (a) 25% of 60 kg,   (b) 5% of £900.

3 In an examination Felicity scored 75% of the marks and Daisy scored $\frac{4}{5}$ of the marks.
Who has the better score?
Give a reason for your answer.

4 What is (a) 60 pence as a percentage of £3,
(b) 15 seconds as a percentage of 1 minute?

5 In a survey, 500 people were questioned about things they recycled.
25% of the people said they recycled paper.
How many people is this?

Edexcel

6 A pop concert is attended by 35 000 people.
2% of the people are given a free T-shirt.
How many people are given a free T-shirt?

7 Jimmy is given £4 pocket money.
He spends 15% of it on a magazine.
How much was the magazine?

8 The total cost of the orange juice for 50 drinks is £37.50.
Each glass of drink is sold at a 20% profit.
Work out the price at which each glass of orange juice is sold.

9 Maggie normally works Monday to Friday and is paid £6.50 per hour.
When she works on a Saturday she is paid 30% **more**.
How much is she paid per hour for working on a Saturday?

10 Harvey sees this advertisement.
Calculate the actual price of the language course.

FRENCH language course

45% off the recommended price of £57

11 A pogo stick is bought for £12.50 and sold for £8.
What is the percentage loss?

12 A farmer has 200 sheep.
90% of the sheep have lambs.
Of the sheep which have lambs 45% have two lambs.
How many of the sheep have two lambs?

13

MEGA ACE GAMES SYSTEM
Normal Price £320
Sale Price   £272

Find the percentage reduction on the
Mega Ace Games System in the sale.

Edexcel

14 For safety, the maximum a caravan should weigh is 85% of the tow car.
The Keenan's family car weighs 1124 kg.
(a) Find, to the nearest kg, the maximum weight
of the caravan that the Keenan's car can tow
within the 85% limit.

The Jones's family car weighs 1220 kg and their caravan weighs 1030 kg.
(b) Work out what percentage the caravan is of the car's weight and state whether it is within
the 85% limit.

Edexcel

15 At the beginning of the year the value of car A was £3000 and the value of car B was £15 000.
At the end of the year the value of car A is £2400 and the value of car B is £12 150.
Which car has the larger percentage loss?
Show your working.

16 In 2002, the population of the World was estimated to be 6340 million.
If the population increases at the rate of 1.7% per year, estimate the population of the World in 2005.
Give your answer correct to 3 significant figures.

17 A clothes shop has a sale.
All the original prices are reduced by 24% to give the sale price.
The sale price of a jacket is £36.86.
Work out the original price of the jacket.   Edexcel

18 A shop buys Indian rugs from a factory.
In July, the cost to the shop of buying a rug was £100.
The shop bought 800 rugs in July.
In August, the cost to the shop of buying a rug increased by 10%.
The number of rugs bought by the shop decreased by 25%.
Find the difference between the total cost to the shop of all the rugs bought in July and the total cost of all the rugs bought by the shop in August.   Edexcel

19

1st STOP Car Insurance
Typical insurance:
Vauxhall Corsa - £650 per year
No Claims Discount Available

(a) Vanessa has a Vauxhall Corsa. She is given a no claims discount.
After taking off her no claims discount she has to pay £390 to insure her car.
Calculate her no claims discount as a percentage of £650.

(b) Cedric has a BMW car. He is given a 65% no claims discount.
After the discount he has to pay £336 to insure his car.
Calculate the price of the insurance before the discount.

20 This report appeared in a motoring magazine.

> In the first year of ownership a new car loses 20% of its value
> and in the second year it loses 15% of its one-year old value.

If this report is true, what is the percentage loss in the value of a new car in its first 2 years?

21 Questionnaires were sent to a number of people.
72 people replied.
This was only 18% of all the people that had been sent questionnaires.
How many people had been sent questionnaires?

22 A greengrocer buys apples and resells them at a profit of 12%.
How much did the greengrocer pay for apples which are sold for 84 pence?

23 Alan sells his bicycle to Paul and makes a 25% loss.
Paul then sells the bicycle to Joe for £49.50 and makes a 10% profit.
How much did Alan pay for the bicycle?

What you need to know

- Time can be given using either the **12-hour clock** or the **24-hour clock**.

  Eg 1 (a) 1120 is equivalent to 11.20 am.
  (b) 1645 is equivalent to 4.45 pm.

  > When using the 12-hour clock:
  > times **before** midday are given as am,
  > times **after** midday are given as pm.

- **Timetables** are usually given using the 24-hour clock.

- **Hourly pay** is paid at a **basic rate** for a fixed number of hours.
  Overtime pay is usually paid at a higher rate such as time and a half, which means each hour's work is worth 1.5 times the basic rate.

- Everyone is allowed to earn some money which is not taxed. This is called a **tax allowance**.

- Tax is only paid on income earned in excess of the tax allowance. This is called **taxable income**.

  Eg 2 Tom earns £5800 per year. His tax allowance is £4615 per year and he pays tax at 10p in the £ on his taxable income. Find how much income tax Tom pays per year.

  Taxable income = £5800 − £4615 = £1185
  Income tax payable = £1185 × 0.10 = £118.50

  > First find the taxable income, then multiply taxable income by rate in £.

- **Value added tax**, or **VAT**, is a tax on some goods and services and is added to the bill.

- When considering a **best buy**, compare quantities by using the same units.

  Eg 3 Peanut butter is available in small or large jars.
  Small jar: 250 grams for 68 pence   Large jar: 454 grams for £1.25
  Which size is the better value for money?

  Small jar: 250 ÷ 68 = 3.67... grams per penny
  Large jar: 454 ÷ 125 = 3.63... grams per penny
  The small jar gives more grams per penny and is better value.

  > Compare the number of grams per penny for each size.

- Money invested in a savings account at a bank or building society earns **interest**.

- With **Simple Interest**, the interest is paid out each year and not added to your account.

  $$\text{Simple Interest} = \frac{\text{Amount}}{\text{invested}} \times \frac{\text{Time in}}{\text{years}} \times \frac{\text{Rate of interest}}{\text{per year}}$$

  Eg 4 Find the Simple Interest paid on £600 invested for 6 months at 8% per year.

  Simple Interest $= 600 \times \frac{6}{12} \times \frac{8}{100} = 600 \times 0.5 \times 0.08 = £24$

- With **Compound Interest**, the interest earned each year is added to your account and also earns interest the following year.

  Eg 5 Find the **Compound Interest** paid on £600 invested for 2 years at 6% per year.

1st year		**2nd year**	
Investment	= £600	Investment	= £636
Interest: £600 × 0.06	= £ 36	Interest: £636 × 0.06	= £ 38.16
Value after one year	= £636	Value after two years	= £674.16

  Compound Interest = Final value − Original value = £674.16 − £600 = £74.16

- **Exchange rates** are used to show what £1 will buy in foreign currencies.

1 The times of rail journeys from Guildford to Waterloo are shown.

Guildford	0703	0722	0730	0733	0749	0752
Worplesdon	0708	0727	—	0739	—	0757
Clapham Junction	0752	—	0800	0822	—	—
Waterloo	0800	0815	0808	0830	0823	0844

(a) Karen catches the 0722 from Guildford to Waterloo.
How many minutes does the journey take?

(b) Graham arrives at Worplesdon station at 0715.
What is the time of the next train to Clapham Junction?

2 Last year Harry paid the following gas bills.

£146.32	£42.87	£36.55	£133.06

This year he will pay his gas bills by 12 equal monthly payments.
Use last year's gas bills to calculate his monthly payments.

3 Felix is paid at time and a half for overtime. His overtime rate of pay is £8.40 per hour.
What is his basic rate of pay?

4 Amrit pays his council tax by 10 instalments.
His first instalment is £143.25 and the other 9 instalments are £137 each.
How much is his total council tax?

5 Nick is on holiday in Spain.
He hires a car at the rates shown.

There are 1.60 euros to £1.

Nick hires the car for 5 days and drives
it for a total of 720 kilometres.
Calculate the total cost of hiring the car.
Give your answer in pounds.

CAR HIRE

Daily rate	54 euros
Free kilometres per day	120
Excess kilometre charge	0.60 euros

6 Members of the Art Club at Oldcastle School wish to hire a coach for a day trip to London and back.
There are two possible firms to hire from, Northlands and Eastline.
The total cost to hire the coach from Northlands is £562.80, which consists of a fixed charge of £100 and a charge of 52p per kilometre.

(a) (i) How many kilometres is the journey to London and back?
(ii) Given that 1 kilometre is 0.62 miles, change your answer into miles.

Eastline charge £1 per mile and make no fixed charge.

(b) Calculate the **saving** which the club would make by hiring from Eastline instead of Northlands?

Edexcel

7 Mrs Tilsed wishes to buy a car priced at £2400.

Two options are available.
Option 1 – A deposit of 20% of £2400 and 24 monthly payments of £95.
Option 2 – For a single payment the dealer offers a discount of 5% on £2400.

How much more does it cost to buy the car if option 1 is chosen rather than option 2?

8 Angela is paid £5.40 per hour for a basic 35-hour week. Overtime is paid at time and a half.
One week Angela worked $37\frac{1}{2}$ hours.
How much did Angela earn that week?

9 Leroy earns £13 600 per year.
He has a tax allowance of £4615 and pays tax at the rate of 10p in the £ on the first £1920 of his taxable income and 22p in the £ on the remainder.
How much income tax does he pay each year?

10 The table below shows the cost of hiring a wallpaper stripper.

Cost for the first day	Extra cost per day for each additional day
£7.50	£2.50

Vivian hires the wallpaper stripper.
The total cost of hiring the wallpaper stripper was £35.
How many days did Vivian hire it for?

11 Sam wants to buy a Hooper washing machine.
Hooper washing machines are sold in three different shops.

Washing Power	Whytes	Clean Up
$\frac{1}{4}$ OFF usual price of £330	20% OFF usual price of £320	£210 plus VAT at 17½%

Work out the cost of the washing machine in each shop.

Edexcel

12 Reg travels to Ireland. The exchange rate is 1.60 euros to the £.
(a) He changes £40 into euros.
How many euros does he receive?
(b) A taxi fare costs 10 euros.
What is the cost of the taxi fare in pounds and pence?

13 Toffee is sold in bars of two sizes.
A large bar weighs 450 g and costs £1.69. A small bar weighs 275 g and costs 99p.
Which size of bar is better value for money?
You must show all your working.

14 Lily invests £1000 at 4.25% per annum simple interest.
She withdraws her money after 6 months.
How much interest did she get?

15 Nesta invests £508 in a bank account paying compound interest at a rate of 10% per annum.
Calculate the total amount in Nesta's bank account after 2 years.

Edexcel

16 The price of a new television is £423. This price includes Value Added Tax at $17\frac{1}{2}$%.
(a) Work out the cost of the television **before** VAT was added.

By the end of each year, the value of a television has fallen by 12% of its value at the start of that year.
The value of a television was £423 at the start of the first year.
(b) Work out the value of the television at the end of the **third** year.
Give your answer to the nearest penny.

Edexcel

17 (a) Mike invests £3000 at 5% per annum compound interest.
What is the value of his investment after 3 years?
(b) Jayne invests her money at 6% per annum compound interest.
What is the percentage increase in the value of her investment after 3 years?

What you need to know

● The ratio 3 : 2 is read '3 to 2'.

● A ratio is used only to **compare** quantities.
A ratio does not give information about the exact values of quantities being compared.

● Different forms of the **same ratio**, such as 2 : 1 and 6 : 3, are called **equivalent ratios**.

● In its **simplest form**, a ratio contains whole numbers which have no common factor other than 1.

| Eg 1 | Write £2.40 : 40p in its simplest form.
£2.40 : 40p = 240p : 40p
= 240 : 40
= 6 : 1 |

> All quantities in a ratio must be in the **same units** before the ratio can be simplified.

● You should be able to solve a variety of problems involving ratio.

| Eg 2 | The ratio of bats to balls in a box is 3 : 5.
There are 12 bats in the box.
How many balls are there?

$12 \div 3 = 4$
$3 \times 4 : 5 \times 4 = 12 : 20$
There are 20 balls in the box. |

> For every 3 bats there are 5 balls.
> To find an equivalent ratio to 3 : 5,
> in which the first number is 12,
> multiply each number in the ratio by 4.

| Eg 3 | A wall costs £660 to build.
The costs of materials to labour are in the ratio 4 : 7.
What is the cost of labour?

$4 + 7 = 11$
$£660 \div 11 = £60$
Cost of labour = £60 × 7 = £420 |

> The numbers in the ratio add to 11.
> For every £11 of the total cost, £4 pays for materials and £7 pays for labour.
> So, **divide** by 11 and then **multiply** by 7.

● When two different quantities are always in the **same ratio** the two quantities are in **direct proportion**.

| Eg 4 | 20 litres of petrol cost £14.
Find the cost of 25 litres of petrol.

20 litres cost £14
1 litre costs £14 ÷ 20 = £0.70
25 litres cost £0.70 × 25 = £17.50 |

> This is sometimes called the **unitary method**.
> **Divide** by 20 to find the cost of 1 litre.
> **Multiply** by 25 to find the cost of 25 litres.

Exercise 10   Do not use a calculator for questions 1 to 6.

1 A toy box contains large bricks and small bricks in the ratio 1 : 4.
The box contains 40 bricks. How many large bricks are in the box?

2 To make mortar a builder mixes sand and cement in the ratio 3 : 1.
The builder uses 2.5 kg of cement. How much sand does he use?

3 In a drama club the ratio of boys to girls is 2 : 3.
What fraction of club members are girls?

4 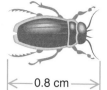 This magnifying glass makes things look bigger.
It enlarges in the ratio 1 : 5.
What is the length of the beetle under the magnifying glass?

Not to scale ← 0.8 cm →

5 Robert used these ingredients to make 24 buns.

> 100 g of butter,   80 g of sugar,   90 g of flour,
> 2 eggs,   30 ml of milk

Robert wants to make 36 similar buns.
Write down how much of each ingredient he
needs for 36 buns.

Edexcel

6 The ratio of men to women playing golf one day is 7 : 3.
(a)   What percentage of the people playing golf are men?
(b)   There are 21 men playing. How many women are playing?

7 Rashid has 35 sweets.
He shares them in the ratio 4 : 3 with his sister.
Rashid keeps the larger share.
How many sweets does Rashid keep?

Edexcel

8 Dec shares a prize of £435 with Annabel in the ratio 3 : 2.
What is the difference in the amount of money they each receive?

9 To make 20 m³ of concrete for a building, the builders use:

4 m³ of cement, 12 m³ of sand and 4 m³ of ballast.

(a)   What is the ratio of cement to sand? Give your answer in its lowest terms.
(b)   How much cement would be needed for 100 m³ of concrete?

Edexcel

10 Two students are talking about their school outing.

> My class went to Tower Bridge last week.
> There are 30 people in my class.
> The total cost was £82.50

> There are 45 people in my group.
> What will be the total cost for my group?

11 Three 1-litre tins of paint cost a total of £26.85.
Find the cost of five of the 1-litre tins of paint.

Edexcel

12 On a map the distance between two towns is 5 cm.
The actual distance between the towns is 1 kilometre.
What is the scale of the map in the form of 1 : n?

13 Malika's father won £128.
He shared the £128 between his three children in the ratio 6 : 3 : 1.
(a)   Malika was given the biggest share. Work out how much money Malika received.
(b)   Malika saved $\frac{2}{3}$ of her share. Work out how much Malika saved.

Edexcel

Speed and Other Compound Measures

What you need to know

- **Speed** is a compound measure because it involves **two** other measures.

- **Speed** is a measurement of how fast something is travelling.
  It involves two other measures, **distance** and **time**.
  In situations where speed is not constant, **average speed** is used.

$$\text{Speed} = \frac{\text{Distance}}{\text{Time}}$$

$$\text{Average speed} = \frac{\text{Total distance travelled}}{\text{Total time taken}}$$

> The formula linking speed, distance and time can be rearranged and remembered as:
> $$S = D \div T$$
> $$D = S \times T$$
> $$T = D \div S$$

- You should be able to solve problems involving speed, distance and time.

  Eg 1 A greyhound takes 32 seconds to run 400 metres.
  Calculate its speed in metres per second.

  $$\text{Speed} = \frac{\text{Distance}}{\text{Time}} = \frac{400}{32} = 12.5 \text{ metres per second}$$

  Eg 2 Norrie says, "If I drive at an average speed of 60 km/h it will take me $2\frac{1}{2}$ hours to complete my journey." What distance is his journey?

  $$\text{Distance} = \text{Speed} \times \text{Time} = 60 \times 2\frac{1}{2} = 150 \text{ km}$$

  Eg 3 Ellen cycles 5 km at an average speed of 12 km/h.
  How many minutes does she take?

  > To change hours to minutes:
  > **multiply by 60**

  $$\text{Time} = \frac{\text{Distance}}{\text{Speed}} = \frac{5}{12} \text{ hours} = \frac{5}{12} \times 60 = 25 \text{ minutes}$$

- **Distance-time graphs** are used to illustrate journeys.

  > On a distance-time graph:
  > Speed can be calculated from the gradient of a line.
  > The faster the speed the steeper the gradient.
  > Zero gradient (horizontal line) means zero speed.

  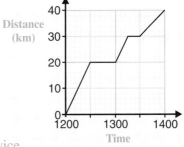

  Eg 4 The graph shows a car journey.
  - (a) How many times does the car stop?
  - (b) (i) Between what times does the car travel fastest?
    Explain your answer.
    - (ii) What is the speed of the car during this part of the journey?

  - (a) Twice
  - (b) (i) 1200 to 1230.
    Steepest gradient.
    - (ii) $\text{Speed} = \dfrac{\text{Distance}}{\text{Time}} = \dfrac{20 \text{ km}}{\frac{1}{2} \text{ hour}} = 40 \text{ km/h}$

- **Density** is a compound measure which involves the measures **mass** and **volume**.

  Eg 5 A block of metal has mass 500 g and volume 400 cm³.

  $$\text{Density} = \frac{\text{Mass}}{\text{Volume}} = \frac{500}{400} = 1.25 \text{ g/cm}^3$$

  > $$\text{Density} = \frac{\text{Mass}}{\text{Volume}}$$

- **Population density** is a measure of how populated an area is.

  Eg 6 The population of Cumbria is 489 700.
  The area of Cumbria is 6824 km².

  > $$\text{Population density} = \frac{\text{Population}}{\text{Area}}$$

  $$\text{Population density} = \frac{\text{Population}}{\text{Area}} = \frac{489\,700}{6824} = 71.8 \text{ people/km}^2.$$

Do not use a calculator for questions 1 to 5.

1 Norma travels 128 km in 2 hours.
Calculate her average speed in kilometres per hour.

2 Sean cycled 24 km at an average speed of 16 km/h.
How long did he take to complete the journey?

3 Ahmed takes $2\frac{1}{2}$ hours to drive from New Milton to London.
He averages 66 km/h. What distance does he drive?

4 Nigel runs 4 km at an average speed of 6 km/h.
How many minutes does he take?

5 A lorry travels 24 miles in 30 minutes.
Calculate the average speed of the lorry in miles per hour.

6 Gail leaves home at 0950 to walk to the park.
She walks at an average speed of 5 km/h and reaches the park at 1020.
How far is the park from her home?

7 The diagram shows the distances, in miles, between some junctions on a motorway.

A coach is travelling west.
At 1040 it passes junction 27 and at 1052 it passes junction 26.
(a) Calculate the average speed of the coach in miles per hour.

Between junctions 26 and 25 the coach travels at an average speed of 30 miles per hour.
(b) Calculate the time when the coach passes junction 25.

8 Ken and Wendy go from home to their caravan site.
The caravan site is 50 km from their home.
Ken goes on his bike. Wendy drives in her car.
The diagram shows information about the journeys they made.

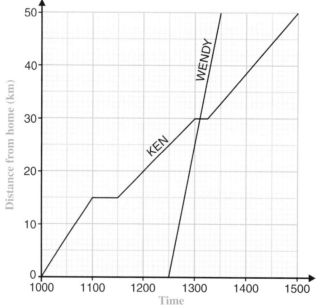

(a) At what time did Wendy pass Ken?
(b) Between which two times was Ken cycling at his greatest speed?
(c) Work out Wendy's average speed for her journey.

Edexcel

9 Jon cycled a distance of 18 km from Guildford to Cranleigh.
The graph shows Jon's cycle ride.
On the way, Jon stopped to buy a drink at a shop.

(a) (i) Write down the distance of the shop from Guildford.
    (ii) Write down the time at which Jon stopped.
    (iii) For how long did he stop?

Jon stayed at Cranleigh for lunch.
He left Cranleigh at 1.30 pm.
He cycled back to Guildford at a steady speed.
He reached Guildford at 3 pm.

(b) Work out the steady speed at which he cycled back to Guildford.

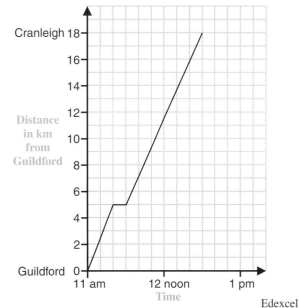

Edexcel

10 On Monday it took Helen 40 minutes to drive to work.
On Tuesday it took Helen 25 minutes to drive to work.
Her average speed on Monday was 18 miles per hour.
What was her average speed on Tuesday?

11 A coach leaves Gateshead at 0830 to travel to London.
It completes the first 270 km of the journey at 90 km/hour before stopping at a service station.
The coach stops at the service station for 30 minutes.
After leaving the service station the coach travels a further 180 km, arriving in London at 1500.

(a) Draw a distance-time graph for the coach journey.
Use a scale of 2 cm for 1 hour on the horizontal axis and 1 cm for 50 km on the vertical axis.

(b) What is the average speed of the coach from the service station to London?

Travis leaves London at 1000 and travels by car to Gateshead on the same route.

(c) Travis gets to the service station as the coach is about to leave.
At what average speed is Travis driving?

12 In the College Games, Michael Jackson won the 200 metres race in a time of 20.32 seconds.
Calculate his average speed in metres per second. Give your answer correct to 1 decimal place.

Edexcel

13 A copper statue has a mass of 1080 g and a volume of 120 cm³.
Work out the density of copper.

14 A silver medal has a mass of 200 g. The density of silver is 10.5 g/cm³.
What is the volume of the medal?

15 The population of Jamaica is 2.8 million people. The area of Jamaica is 10 800 km².
What is the population density of Jamaica?

16 The table gives some information about North America.

Country	Area (km²)	Population	Population density (people/km²)
Canada	9 860 000		2.98
United States		2.68×10^8	28.9

(a) Calculate the population of Canada.   (b) Calculate the area of the United States.
Give your answers to 3 significant figures.

Speed and Other Compound Measures

Section Review - Number

Do not use a calculator for questions 1 to 26.

1 Work out $40 \times 50 \times 500$. Give your answer in words.

2 Calculate. (a) 256×37 (b) $925 \div 37$

3 (a) 4 litres of milk costs £1.96. How much is 1 litre of milk?
  (b) Apples cost 84 pence per kilogram. What is the cost of 5 kilograms of apples?

4 Use these numbers to answer the following questions.
  2   12   27   36   80   88
  (a) Which number is a factor of 16?   (b) Which number is a multiple of 16?
  (c) Which number is a prime number?   (d) Which number is a square number?
  (e) Which number is a cube number?

5 To buy a car, Ricky has to pay 24 monthly payments of £198.
How much does he have to pay altogether to buy the car?

6 The lowest temperatures recorded in Manchester each night for a week are given.
  $7°C$, $-4°C$, $3°C$, $1°C$, $-2°C$, $0°C$, $-1°C$
  (a) Write down the temperatures in order. Start with the lowest temperature.
  (b) Work out the difference between the highest and lowest temperatures.

7 You want to estimate the value of 21.2×31.2.
Each number must be written to 1 significant figure.
  (a) Write down a suitable calculation which could be used.
  (b) State the value of this estimate.

8
SUPER ACE GAMES SYSTEM
Normal Price £120
Sale Price $\frac{1}{3}$ off

Work out the sale price of the
Super Ace Games System.

9 (a) Write these decimals in order, from smallest to largest.
      0.345   0.35 -0.4 0.355 -0.35
  (b) Write down a decimal that lies halfway between 0.4 and 0.5.
  (c) Work out (i) $5 - 0.26$,   (ii) 0.2×0.4,   (iii) $24 \div 0.3$.
  (d) A turkey costs £2.40 per kilogram.
      What is the cost of a turkey which weighs 6.5 kilograms?

10 (a) Work out (i) 10^5,   (ii) $10^2 - 2^5$,   (iii) $2^3 \times 3^2$,   (iv) $30^2 \div 10^3$.
  (b) Which is smaller, 5^4 or 4^5? Show **all** your working.
  (c) Work out $\sqrt{25} \times \sqrt{100}$.

11 (a) Write $\frac{4}{5}$ as a percentage.
  (b) Find 25% of £500.
  (c) Nora gets 26 out of 40 in a test. What percentage of the marks did she get?

12 (a) Write these fractions in ascending order: $\frac{1}{2}$ $\frac{2}{3}$ $\frac{3}{5}$ $\frac{5}{8}$ $\frac{3}{4}$
  (b) Write down a fraction that lies halfway between $\frac{1}{5}$ and $\frac{1}{4}$.
  (c) Work out (i) $\frac{1}{4} + \frac{2}{5}$,   (ii) $\frac{2}{3} - \frac{1}{2}$,   (iii) $\frac{4}{5} \times \frac{2}{3}$.
  (d) Work out $\frac{2}{5}$ of 12.

13 A crowd of 54 000 people watch a carnival.
  (a) 15% of the crowd are men. How many men watch the carnival?
  (b) Two-thirds of the crowd are children. How many children watch the carnival?

14 (a) Given that $59 \times 347 = 20\,473$, find the exact value of $\frac{20\,473}{590}$.
  (b) Use approximations to estimate the value of 49×302.
     Show all your working.

15 (a) Diesel costs £0.75 per litre in England. Calculate the cost of 45 litres of diesel.
  (b) In France, diesel is 20% cheaper than in England.
     Calculate the cost of 45 litres of diesel in France.

16 Mr. Smithson insures the contents of his house.
  He has to pay £2.10 per £1000 of the value of the contents.
  His house contents are valued at £26 500.
  Calculate how much his insurance costs.   Edexcel

17 The price of a box of chocolates is £4.32.
  There are 24 chocolates in the box.

  Buy **one** box of chocolates for £4.32
  Buy a **second** box of chocolates for half price.

  (a) Work out the cost of **one** chocolate.

  George buys two boxes of chocolates
  on the special offer.
  (b) Work out the total amount George should pay for the two boxes of chocolates.

  18 of the chocolates in a box are milk chocolates.
  (c) Work out 18 as a percentage of 24.   Edexcel

18 Two lettuces and three cucumbers cost £2.67.
  Cucumbers cost 59p each.
  How much does a lettuce cost?

19 Three cups of tea cost £2.85. How much will five cups of tea cost?

20 It costs £1.20 to buy a melon on Tuesday.
  On Wednesday it costs 15% **more**.
  How much does it cost to buy a melon on Wednesday?

21 (a) Conrad cycles 24 km in $1\frac{1}{2}$ hours. What is his cycling speed in kilometres per hour?
  (b) Cas cycles 24 km at 15 km/h. She sets off at 0930. At what time does she finish?

22 Jean uses 36 balls of wool to knit a black and white jumper.
  The ratio of black wool to white wool is 7 : 2.
  How many balls of black wool are used?

23 Jack shares £180 between his two children Ruth and Ben.
  The ratio of Ruth's share to Ben's share is 5 : 4.
  (a) Work out how much each child is given.

  Ben then gives 10% of his share to Ruth.
  (b) Work out the percentage of the £180 that Ruth now has.   Edexcel

24 The prime factors of a certain number are $2^3 \times 3 \times 11$. What is the number?   Edexcel

25 (a) Write 72 as a product of its prime factors.
  (b) Write 96 as a product of its prime factors.
  (c) Hence find the least common multiple of 72 and 96.

26 (a) Write 4×10^5 as an ordinary number.
  (b) Multiply 4×10^5 by 6×10^3. Give your answer in standard form.

27 Fred won a prize of £12 000.
He put some of the money in a Building Society.
He put the rest of the money in the Post Office.
The money was put in the Building Society and Post Office in the ratio 2 : 3.
(a) Calculate the amount of money put in the Building Society.

After a number of years the money put in the Building Society had increased by 9%.
(b) Calculate the amount of money Fred then had in the Building Society.

After the same number of years the money Fred had put in the Post Office had increased by an eighth.
(c) Calculate the increase in the amount of money in the Post Office.

Edexcel

28 Ken drives from his home to the city centre.
The graph represents his journey.

(a) How long did Ken take to reach the city centre?

(b) How far from the city centre does Ken live?

(c) What is his average speed for the journey in kilometres per hour?

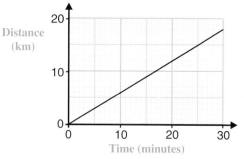

29 (a) Write the following fractions as decimals, writing all the figures shown on your calculator.
(i) $\frac{9}{10}$ (ii) $\frac{45}{51}$

(b) Work out a fraction that is between $\frac{9}{10}$ and $\frac{45}{51}$ in size.

Edexcel

30 Harvey lives 3 kilometres from school. He walks to school at an average speed of 5 km/h.
The school day starts at 0900.
What is the latest time Harvey can leave home and still get to school on time?

31 Evaluate $\dfrac{(23.4 + 35.6) \times 5.7}{200.3 \times (16.2 - 8.15)}$

Edexcel

32 In England, a jar of **extra fruity** apricot jam weighs 454 g and costs 89p.
In France, a jar of **extra fruity** apricot jam weighs 681 g and costs 1.84 euros.
£1 = 1.58 euros.
In which country is the jam better value for money?
You must show all your working.

33 There are 12 inches in 1 foot. There are 3 feet in 1 yard. There are 2.54 centimetres in 1 inch.
Express 1 metre in yards. Give your answer correct to 3 decimal places.

Edexcel

34 (a) What is the reciprocal of 0.25? (b) Work out $\dfrac{3.2^2}{\sqrt{0.04}}$.

35 A caravan is for sale at £7200.
Stuart buys the caravan on credit.
The credit terms are:

> deposit 25% of sale price and 36 monthly payments of £175.

Express the extra amount paid for credit, compared with the cash price, as a percentage of the cash price.

36 In 2000, Ashley's council tax bill was £905.48.
In 2001, Ashley's council tax bill was 6.8% more than in 2000.
In 2002, Ashley's council tax bill was 11.9% more than in 2001.
Calculate Ashley's council tax bill in 2002.
Give your answer to a suitable degree of accuracy.

SR

37 The number 10^{100} is called a googol.
(a) Write the number 50 googols in standard index form.

A nanometre is 10^{-9} metres.
(b) Write 50 nanometres, in metres.
Give your answer in standard index form. Edexcel

38 £1 can buy 1.54 euros. £1 can buy 1.37 dollars.
How many dollars can be bought with 1000 euros?

39 (a) Place the following numbers in descending order.

$\sqrt{6.9}$ 2.58 1.6^2 $2\frac{4}{7}$

(b) (i) Calculate $\frac{612 \times 29.6}{81.3 - 18.9}$.
Give your answer correct to 3 significant figures.
(ii) Use approximations to show that your answer is about right.
Show all your working.

40 The selling price of a computer is the **list price** plus VAT at $17\frac{1}{2}\%$.
The **list price** of a computer is £786.
(a) Work out the selling price of the computer.

The selling price of another computer is £1292.50.
(b) Work out the **list price** of this computer. Edexcel

41 $P = 4 \times 10^5$ and $Q = 5 \times 10^{-2}$.
Calculate (a) $P \times Q$, (b) $P \div Q$, (c) Q^2
Give your answers in standard form.

42 $p = 3^2 \times 5 \times 7$ and $q = 2 \times 3 \times 5^2$. Find the least common multiple of p and q.

43 (a) You are given the formula $k = \frac{3}{4}m^2$.
Calculate the exact value of k, when $m = 4.8 \times 10^3$. Give your answer in standard form.
(b) Calculate $\sqrt{\frac{5.2 \times 10^{-3}}{(0.039)^2}}$, correct to two decimal places.

44 (a) Jools invests £2000 at 6.5% per annum compound interest.
Calculate the value of his investment at the end of 3 years.
(b) Jennifer gets 6% per annum on her investment.
After one year the value of her investment is £1272.
How much did she invest?

45 Last year Alf had a tax allowance of £4615 and paid £4328 in tax.
The rates of tax were:

10p in the £ on the first £1920 of taxable income and
22p in the £ on all the remaining taxable income.

How much did Alf earn last year?

46 The surface area of the Earth is approximately 5.05×10^8 square kilometres.
The surface area of the Earth covered by water is approximately 3.57×10^8 square kilometres.

(a) Calculate the surface area of the Earth not covered by water.
Give your answer in standard form.
(b) What percentage of the Earth's surface is not covered by water?
Give your answer to an appropriate degree of accuracy.

Section Review . . . Section Review . . .

Introduction to Algebra

What you need to know

- You should be able to write **algebraic expressions**.

  Eg 1 An expression for the cost of 6 pens at n pence each is $6n$ pence.

  Eg 2 An expression for 2 pence more than n pence is $n + 2$ pence.

- Be able to **simplify expressions** by collecting **like terms** together.

  Eg 3 (a) $2d + 3d = 5d$ (b) $3x + 2 - x + 4 = 2x + 6$ (c) $x + 2x + x^2 = 3x + x^2$

- Be able to **multiply expressions** together.

  Eg 4 (a) $2a \times a = 2a^2$ (b) $y \times y \times y = y^3$ (c) $3m \times 2n = 6mn$

- Recall and use these properties of powers:
  Powers of the same base are **added** when terms are **multiplied**.
  Powers of the same base are **subtracted** when terms are **divided**.
  Powers are **multiplied** when a power is raised to a power.

  $$a^m \times a^n = a^{m+n}$$
  $$a^m \div a^n = a^{m-n}$$
  $$(a^m)^n = a^{m \times n}$$

  Eg 5 (a) $x^3 \times x^2 = x^5$ (b) $a^5 \div a^2 = a^3$ (c) $6m^6 \div 2m^2 = 3m^4$ (d) $(x^2)^3 = x^6$

- How to **multiply out brackets**.

  Eg 6 (a) $2(x - 5) = 2x - 10$ (b) $x(x - 5) = x^2 - 5x$ (c) $2m(m + 3) = 2m^2 + 6m$

- How to **factorise expressions**.

  Eg 7 (a) $3x - 6 = 3(x - 2)$ (b) $m^2 + 5m = m(m + 5)$ (c) $3a^2 - 6a = 3a(a - 2)$

Exercise 12

1 A calculator costs £9.
Write an expression for the cost of k calculators.

2 Godfrey is 5 years older than Mary.
Write expressions for the following

   (a) Godfrey's age when Mary is t years old.
   (b) Mary's age when Godfrey is x years old.

3 A cup of coffee costs x pence and a cup of tea costs y pence.
Write an expression for the cost of 3 cups of coffee and 2 cups of tea.

4 Simplify   (a) $m + 2m + 3m$,   (b) $2m + 2 - m$,   (c) $m \times m \times m$.

5 Simplify   (a) $5x + 3x - x$,   (b) $4y - 3 + 3y - 2$.   Edexcel

6 A muffin costs $d + 3$ pence.
Write an expression for the cost of 5 muffins.

7 Write an expression, in terms of x, for the sum of the angles in this shape.

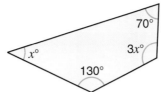

8 Simplify (a) $5a \times 2a$, (b) $3g \times 2h$, (c) $6k \div 3$, (d) $3m \div m$.

9 Which algebraic expressions are equivalent?

| $a + a$ | $2(a + 1)$ | $2a + 1$ | $2a + 2$ | a^3 |

| a^2 | $a + a + 1$ | $2a$ | $a + a + a$ | $a \times a$ |

10 (a) Simplify   (i) $2x + 3 + x$,   (ii) $2x + y - x + y$.
   (b) Multiply out   (i) $2(x + 3)$,   (ii) $x(x - 1)$.
   (c) Multiply out and simplify (i) $2(x - 1) - 3$, (ii) $7 + 3(2 + x)$.
   (d) Factorise   (i) $2a - 6$,   (ii) $x^2 + 2x$.

11 (a) Ken works x hours a week for £y per hour.
      Write an expression for the amount he earns each week.
   (b) Sue works 5 hours less than Ken each week and earns £y per hour.
      Write an expression for the amount Sue earns each week.

12 (a) Simplify $2ab + 3a - 2b + b - 5a + ab$.
   (b) Multiply out and simplify $3(2x + 3) + 2(5 + x)$.

13 Ahmed and Hussein are two brothers. Ahmed is older than Hussein.
   Given that Ahmed's age is $(5x - 4)$ years and Hussein's age is $(2x + 1)$ years,
   write down an expression, in terms of x, for how much older Ahmed is than Hussein.
   Simplify your answer.   Edexcel

14 Simplify. (a) $y^3 \times y^2$ (b) $x^6 \div x^3$ (c) $\dfrac{z^4 \times z}{z^3}$ (d) $(y^3)^2$

15 (a) Multiply out $t^2(t^3 - t^4)$.
   (b) Multiply out and simplify $3(2a + 6) - 2(3a - 6)$.
   (c) Simplify $\dfrac{12a^2b}{4ab}$.   Edexcel

16 Factorise completely (a) $x^2 - 3x$, (b) $2p^2q + pq^2$.   Edexcel

17 (a) Simplify $5 - 3(2n - 1)$.
   (b) Multiply out $(-3m) \times (-2m)$.
   (c) Factorise fully $8mn - 2m$.

18 Simplify (a) $2a^3 \times 3a$, (b) $6x^8 \div 3x^2$, (c) $\dfrac{3m^2 \times 4n^6}{6mn^2}$, (d) $4x^3y \times 5x^2y$.

19 (a) Expand the brackets. (i) $2x(x - 3y)$ (ii) $3a(3a + a^2)$
   (b) Factorise.   (i) $4xy - 2y^2$ (ii) $3m^2 - 12m$
   (c) Simplify. $2x^2 - x(1 + x)$

20 Simplify fully. $\dfrac{4a^2b^3 \times 3a^3b}{6a^5b^2}$.

21 (a) Multiply out $2x(2y - xy)$.
   (b) Factorise $6pq - 3pq^2$.
   (c) Simplify $21m^6 \div 7m^3$.

Solving Equations

What you need to know

- The solution of an equation is the value of the unknown letter that fits the equation.

- You should be able to solve simple equations by **inspection**.

  Eg 1   (a) $a + 2 = 5$ (b) $m - 3 = 7$ (c) $2x = 10$
              $a = 3$ $m = 10$ $x = 5$

- Be able to solve simple problems by **working backwards**.

  Eg 2   I think of a number, multiply it by 3 and add 4. The answer is 19.

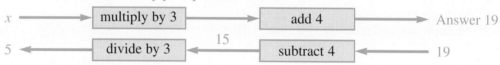

  The number I thought of is 5.

- Be able to use the **balance method** to solve equations.

  Eg 3   Solve these equations.

  (a) $d - 13 = -5$ (b) $-4a = 20$ (c) $5 - 4n = -1$
       $d = -5 + 13$ $a = \frac{20}{-4}$ $-4n = -6$
       $d = 8$ $a = -5$ $n = 1.5$

- Be able to solve equations with unknowns on both sides of the equals sign.

  Eg 4   Solve $3x + 1 = x + 7$.

  $$3x = x + 6$$
  $$2x = 6$$
  $$x = 3$$

- Be able to solve equations which include brackets.

  Eg 5   Solve $4(3 + 2x) = 5(x + 2)$.

  $$12 + 8x = 5x + 10$$
  $$8x = 5x - 2$$
  $$3x = -2$$
  $$x = -\tfrac{2}{3}$$

- Be able to solve equations which involve fractions.

  Eg 6   Solve $\frac{x}{2} + \frac{2x}{3} = 7$.

  $$6 \times \tfrac{x}{2} + 6 \times \tfrac{2x}{3} = 6 \times 7$$
  $$3x + 4x = 42$$
  $$7x = 42$$
  $$x = 6$$

  Eg 7   Solve $\frac{x - 1}{3} = \frac{x + 1}{4}$.

  $$4(x - 1) = 3(x + 1)$$
  $$4x - 4 = 3x + 3$$
  $$4x = 3x + 7$$
  $$x = 7$$

- You should be able to write, or form, equations using the information given in a problem.

Exercise 13

1 What number should be put in the box to make each of these statements correct?

(a) $\boxed{} - 6 = 9$ (b) $2 + \boxed{} = 11$ (c) $4 \times \boxed{} = 20$ (d) $\boxed{} \times 3 - 5 = 7$

2 Solve these equations.

(a) $7 + x = 12$ (b) $5 - x = 3$ (c) $5x = 10$ (d) $5x - 9 = 11$

3 (a) I think of a number, add 3, and then multiply by 2.
　　The answer is 16. What is my number?
(b) I think of a number, double it and then subtract 3.
　　The answer is 5. What is my number?

4 Solve these equations.　(a) $3x - 7 = 23$　　　　(b) $5 + 7x = 47$
　　　　　　　　　　　　(c) $5(x - 2) = 20$　　　(d) $3x - 7 = x + 15$

5 The lengths of these rods are given, in centimetres, in terms of n.

 n　　　　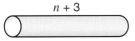 $n + 3$　　　　$2n - 1$

The total length of the rods is 30 cm.
By forming an equation, find the value of n.

6 Mandy buys a small box of chocolates and a large box of chocolates.
The diagram shows the number of chocolates in each box.

Altogether there are 47 chocolates.
By forming an equation, find the number
of chocolates in the larger box.

n　　　　　$2n + 5$
chocolates　chocolates

7 Solve these equations.　(a) $7x + 4 = 60$　　　(b) $3x - 7 = -4$
　　　　　　　　　　　　(c) $2(x + 3) = -2$　　(d) $3x - 4 = 1 + x$

8 Solve these equations.
(a) $3y + 7 = 28$　　(b) $2(3p + 2) = 19$　　(c) $3t - 4 = 5t - 10$　　Edexcel

9 Solve.
(a) $4a + 3 = 9$　　(b) $5b - 7 = 2b + 5$　　(c) $3(c - 6) = 10 - 2c$　　Edexcel

10 Solve these equations.　(a) $\frac{x}{3} = -7$　　　　(b) $2(x - 1) = 3$
　　　　　　　　　　　　(c) $5 - 2x = 3x + 2$　　(d) $\frac{1}{4}x + 5 = 2$

11 Solve the equations　(a) $5(2p - 3) = 50$,　　(b) $\frac{16 - q}{3} = 3$.　　Edexcel

12 Solve these equations.
(a) $\frac{x + 5}{2} = 3$　　(b) $\frac{1 - 2x}{3} = 2$　　(c) $\frac{3}{2} = \frac{3x}{5}$　　(d) $\frac{x}{2} + \frac{x}{3} = 5$

13
$$A \vdash \overset{2d}{\quad\quad} \overset{3}{\quad} \overset{2d}{\quad\quad} \dashv B \quad C \vdash \overset{d}{\quad} \overset{5}{\quad} \overset{d}{\quad} \overset{5}{\quad} \dashv D$$
The diagram shows two straight lines AB and CD. Each line is cut into sections.
The length, in centimetres, of each section is shown in the diagram.
(a) Write down, in terms of d,　(i) the length of AB,　(ii) the length of CD.

The length of AB is equal to the length of CD.
(b) (i) Write down an equation in d,
　　(ii) Solve your equation to find the value of d.　　Edexcel

14 Solve these equations.　(a) $2(x - 3) + 3(x + 1) = 2$　(b) $3(2 + 3a) = 5(a - 2)$
　　　　　　　　　　　　(c) $x - 3(x + 1) = 2(5 - 2x)$

15 Solve the equations　(a) $\frac{x - 3}{4} = 1 - x$,　　(b) $\frac{x - 3}{2} = \frac{2x + 1}{3}$.

Formulae

What you need to know

- An **expression** is just an answer using letters and numbers.
  A **formula** is an algebraic rule. It always has an equals sign.

- You should be able to **write simple formulae**.

  Eg 1 | A packet of crisps weighs 25 grams. Write a formula for the total weight, W grams, of n packets of crisps.
  $$W = 25n$$

  Eg 2 | Start with t, add 5 and then multiply by 3. The result is p. Write a formula for p in terms of t.
  $$p = 3(t + 5)$$

- Be able to **substitute** values into given expressions and formulae.

  Eg 3 (a) Find the value of $4x - y$ when $x = 5$ and $y = 7$.
  $$4x - y = 4 \times 5 - 7$$
  $$= 20 - 7$$
  $$= 13$$

  (b) $A = pq - r$
  Find the value of A when $p = 2$, $q = -2$ and $r = 3$.
  $$A = pq - r$$
  $$= 2 \times (-2) - 3$$
  $$= -4 - 3$$
  $$= -7$$

  (c) $M = 2n^2$
  Find the value of M when $n = 3$.
  $$M = 2n^2$$
  $$= 2 \times 3^2$$
  $$= 2 \times 9$$
  $$= 18$$

- Be able to **rearrange** a given formula to make another letter (variable) the subject.

  Eg 4 $y = 2x + a$
  Make x the subject of the formula.
  $$y = 2x + a$$
  $$y - a = 2x$$
  $$\frac{y - a}{2} = x$$
  So, $x = \dfrac{y - a}{2}$

  Eg 5 $T = a + \sqrt{b}$
  Rearrange the formula to give b in terms of T and a.
  $$T = a + \sqrt{b}$$
  $$T - a = \sqrt{b}$$
  $$(T - a)^2 = b$$
  So, $b = (T - a)^2$

Exercise 14

Do not use a calculator for questions 1 to 10.

1 What is the value of $a - 3b$ when $a = 10$ and $b = 2$?

2 What is the value of $2x + y$ when $x = -3$ and $y = 5$?

3 $H = ab - c$. Find the value of H when $a = 2$, $b = -5$ and $c = 3$.

4 Given that $m = -3$ and $n = 5$, find the value of
(a) $m + n$, (b) $m - n$, (c) $n - m$, (d) mn.

5 If $p = 4$ and $q = -5$ find the value of (a) $3pq$, (b) $p^2 + 2q$.

6 $L = 5(p + q)$. Find the value of L when $p = 2$ and $q = -0.4$.

7 $A = b - cd$. Find the value of A when $b = -3$, $c = 2$ and $d = 4$.

8 What is the value of $10y^2$ when $y = 3$?

9 What is the value of $3x^3$ when $x = 2$?

10 $T = ab^2$. Find the value of T when $a = 4$ and $b = -5$.

11 This is how to work out the amount of meat a dog needs to each each day.

| Find what the dog weighs and multiply by 0.04 |

(a) Use m for the amount of meat and w for what the dog weighs.
Write a formula for m in terms of w.

Scamp is a dog that weighs 30 kg.
(b) How much meat does he need to eat each day?   Edexcel

12 A pen costs 25 pence.
A pencil costs 10 pence.
Louisa buys x pens and y pencils. The total cost is C pence.
(a) Write a formula for C in terms of x and y.
(b) Work out the value of y when $C = 250$ and $x = 6$.   Edexcel

13 (a) Write, in symbols, the rule:

| "To find y, double x and add 1." |

(b) Use your rule from part (a) to calculate the value of x when $y = 9$.   Edexcel

14 $c = y - mx$. Calculate the value of c when $y = 4.95$, $m = -0.75$ and $x = 3$.   Edexcel

15 A formula is given as $c = 3t - 5$. Rearrange the formula to give t in terms of c.

16 $s = \frac{1}{2}(u + v)t$. Work out the value of s when $u = 10$, $v = -25$ and $t = 0.5$.   Edexcel

17 Rearrange the formula $n = 3 + mp$ to make m the subject.

18 The diagram shows a solid.
The volume, V, of the solid is given by the formula
$$V = \frac{\pi h}{3}(R^2 + Rr + r^2)$$

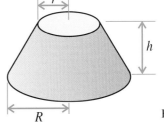

(a) $h = 6.8$, $R = 9.7$ and $r = 5.3$
Calculate the value of V.
Give your answer correct to 3 significant figures.
(b) Make h the subject of the formula.   Edexcel

19 $m = \frac{3}{5}(n - 17)$. Find the value of n when $m = -9$.

20 Make r the subject of the formula $p = \frac{gr}{s}$.

21 You are given the formula $v = u + at$.
(a) Find v when $u = 17$, $a = -8$ and $t = \frac{3}{5}$.
(b) Rearrange the formula to give a in terms of v, u and t.

22 Make s the subject of the formula $t = s^2 + 5$.

23 Make h the subject of the formula $g = \frac{3}{5}h^2$.

24 Make x the subject of the formula $y = \frac{x^2 + 4}{5}$.   Edexcel

Sequences

What you need to know

- A **sequence** is a list of numbers made according to some rule.
  The numbers in a sequence are called **terms**.

- You should be able to draw and continue number sequences represented by patterns of shapes.

  Eg 1 This pattern represents the sequence:
  3, 5, 7, ...

- Be able to continue a sequence by following a given rule.

  Eg 2 The sequence 2, 7, 22, ... is made using the rule:

  > multiply the last number by 3, then add 1.

  The next term in the sequence = $(22 \times 3) + 1 = 66 + 1 = 67$

- Be able to find a rule, and then use it, to continue a sequence.

  > **To continue a sequence:**
  > 1. Work out the rule to get from one term to the next.
  > 2. Apply the same rule to find further terms in the sequence.

  Eg 3 Describe the rule used to make the following sequences.
  Then use the rule to find the next term of each sequence.

  (a) 5, 8, 11, 14, ...   (b) 2, 4, 8, 16, ...   (c) 1, 1, 2, 3, 5, 8, ...
  Rule: Rule: Rule:
  add 3 to last term   multiply last term by 2   add the last two terms
  Next term: 17   Next term: 32   Next term: 13

- Find an expression for the nth term of a sequence.

  > A number sequence which increases (or decreases) by the same amount
  > from one term to the next is called a **linear sequence**.
  > The sequence 2, 8, 14, 20, 26, ...   has a **common difference** of 6.

  Eg 4 Find the nth term of the sequence: 3, 5, 7, 9, ...
  The sequence is linear, common difference = 2.
  To find the nth term add one to the multiples of 2.
  So, the nth term is $2n + 1$.

  > **Special sequences - Square numbers:**   1, 4, 9, 16, 25, ...
  > **Triangular numbers:** 1, 3, 6, 10, 15, ...

Exercise 15

1 What is the next number in each of these sequences?
   (a) 1, 2, 5, 10, ...   (b) 1, 3, 9, 27, ...   (c) 1, $\frac{1}{2}$, $\frac{1}{4}$, $\frac{1}{8}$, ...

2 The first six terms of a sequence are shown. 1, 4, 5, 9, 14, 23, ...
   Write down the next two terms.

3 Look at this sequence of numbers. 2, 5, 8, 11, ...
   (a) What is the next number in the sequence?
   (b) Is 30 a number in this sequence? Give a reason for your answer.

4 The rule for a sequence is:

> Add the last two numbers and divide by 2.

Write down the next three terms when the sequence begins: 3, 7, ...

5 A sequence begins: 5, 15, 45, 135, ...
   (a) Write down the rule, in words, used to get from one term to the next in the sequence.
   (b) Use your rule to find the next term in the sequence.

6 (a) The rule for a sequence of numbers is:

> ADD THE TWO PREVIOUS NUMBERS AND THEN MULTIPLY BY 2

Write down the next two numbers in the sequence: 1, 1, 4, 10, ...
   (b) The first eight numbers in a different sequence of numbers are:

$$3, \ 7, \ 4, \ 8, \ 5, \ 9, \ 6, \ 10, \ ...$$

Write down the next two numbers in the sequence.   Edexcel

7 A sequence begins: 1, 6, 10, 8, ...
The rule to continue the sequence is:

          double the difference between the last two numbers.

Ravi says if you continue the sequence it will end in 0. Is he correct? Explain your answer.

8 The first three patterns in a sequence are shown.

   Pattern 1   **Pattern 2**   **Pattern 3**

   (a) How many squares are in pattern 20?
       Explain how you found your answer.
   (b) Write an expression for the number of squares in the nth pattern.

9 Here are the first four terms of a number sequence: 3, 7, 11, 15.
   (a) Write down the next two terms of the sequence.
   (b) Write down an expression, in terms of n, for the nth term of the sequence.   Edexcel

10 Find the nth term of the following sequences.
   (a) 5, 7, 9, 11, ...   (b) 1, 5, 9, 13, ...

11 Marco writes down a number sequence.
He starts at 120.
Each time he subtracts 12 to get the next number in the sequence.
   (a) Write down the first 5 numbers in the sequence.
   (b) Write down an expression for the nth number in the sequence.   Edexcel

12 (a) Write down the first **three** terms of the sequence whose nth term is given by $n^2 - 4$.
   (b) Will the number 60 be in this sequence? Explain your answer.

13 A sequence begins: 3, 6, 11, 18, 27, ...
   (a) Find the next two terms in this sequence.
   (b) Explain why this is not a linear sequence.
   (c) Explain how you can find the 20th term in the sequence without writing down all the previous terms.

What you need to know

- **Coordinates** (involving positive and negative numbers) are used to describe the position of a point on a graph.

  Eg 1 The coordinates of A are $(-3, 2)$.

  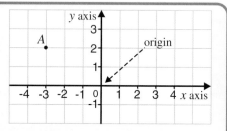

- The x axis is the line $y = 0$.
  The y axis is the line $x = 0$.

- The **gradient** of a line can be found by drawing a right-angled triangle.

  $$\text{Gradient} = \frac{\text{distance up}}{\text{distance along}}$$

  Gradients can be positive, zero or negative.

  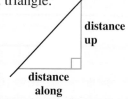

- You should be able to find the equation for a given line.

  In general, the equation of any straight line can be written in the form

  $$y = mx + c$$

  where m is the **gradient** of the line
  and c is the **y-intercept**.

  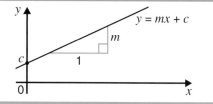

  Eg 2 Find the equation of the line shown on this graph.

  Gradient of line $= \dfrac{\text{distance up}}{\text{distance along}} = \dfrac{2}{1} = 2$

  The graph crosses the y axis at the point $(0, -3)$,
  so the y-intercept is -3.
  The equation of the line is $y = 2x - 3$.

  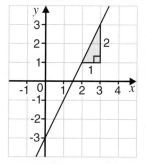

- The points where a line crosses the axes can be found:
  by reading the coordinates from a graph,
  by substituting $x = 0$ and $y = 0$ into the equation of the line.

  Eg 3 The diagram shows a sketch of the line $2y = x + 3$.
  Find the coordinates of the points P and Q.

  When $x = 0$, $2y = 0 + 3$, $2y = 3$, $y = 1\frac{1}{2}$.
  When $y = 0$, $0 = x + 3$, $x = -3$.
  The points are $P\left(0, 1\frac{1}{2}\right)$ and $Q(-3, 0)$.

  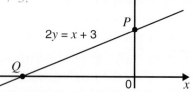

- Equations of the form $px + qy = r$ can be **rearranged** to the form $y = mx + c$.

  Eg 4 The graph of a straight line is given by the equation $4y - 3x = 8$.
  Write this equation in the form $y = mx + c$.
  $4y - 3x = 8$
  $4y = 3x + 8$
  $y = \frac{3}{4}x + 2$

  > The line has gradient $\frac{3}{4}$ and y-intercept 2.

- You should be able to solve equations and problems involving straight line graphs.
- Be able to draw and interpret graphs which represent real-life situations.

1 Draw and label x and y axes from -5 to 4.
(a) On your diagram plot $A\,(4,\,3)$ and $B\,(-5,\,-3)$.
(b) $C\,(p,\,-1)$ is on the line segment AB.
     What is the value of p?

2 (a) Copy and complete this table of values for $y = 2x + 3$.

x	-3	-2	-1	0	1	2
y		-1				

(b) Draw the graph of $y = 2x + 3$ for values of x from -3 to 2.
(c) Use your graph to find (i) the value of y when $x = 1.5$.
                              (ii) the value of x when $y = -0.5$.

Edexcel

3 On the same diagram, draw and label the lines: $y = x + 2$ and $y = 2 - x$, for values of x from -2 to 2.

4 (a) On the same axes, draw the graphs of $y = -2$, $y = x$ and $x + y = 5$.
(b) Which of these lines has a negative gradient?

5 The diagram shows a sketch of the line $2y = 6 - x$.
(a) Find the coordinates of the points P and Q.
(b) The line $2y = 6 - x$ goes through $R\,(-5,\,m)$.
     What is the value of m?

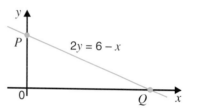

6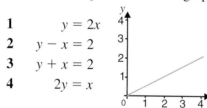

Points P, Q and R are shown on the grid.
(a) Write down the equation of the line PQ.
(b) (i) Use the grid to work out the gradient of the line RP.
     (ii) Write down the equation of the line RP.

7 Match these equations to their graphs.

1 $y = 2x$
2 $y - x = 2$
3 $y + x = 2$
4 $2y = x$

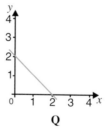 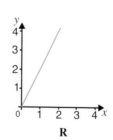 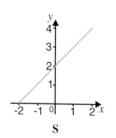

P   Q   R   S

8 (a) Copy and complete the table of values for $2y = 3x - 6$.

x	-2	0	4
y		-3	

(b) Draw the graph of $2y = 3x - 6$ for values of x from -2 to 4.
(c) What is the gradient of the line $2y = 3x - 6$?
(d) Use your graph to find the value of x when $y = 1.5$.

9 The equation of a line is $5y - 2x = 10$.
(a) Write this equation in the form $y = mx + c$.
(b) Write down the equation of the line, parallel to $5y - 2x = 10$, which passes through the point $(0,\,-1)$.

10 The graph shows the cost, in pounds, of electricity used by one person.
The cost is made up of a fixed standing charge, plus the cost of the number of units of electricity used.

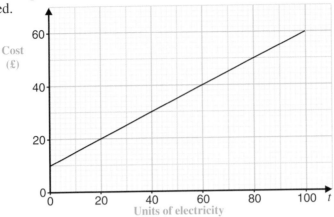

Use the graph to find   (a)   the standing charge in pounds.
                        (b)   the cost, in pence, of one unit of electricity.   Edexcel

11 Errol's house has a meter which measures the amount of water he uses.
The graph can be used to find out how much he must pay for the number of water units that he uses.

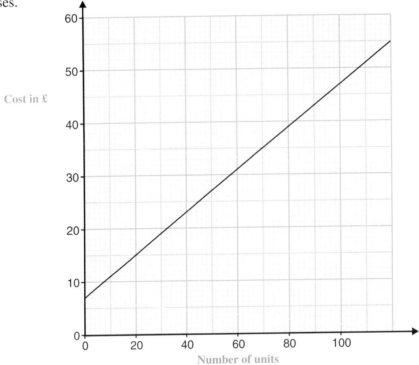

(a)   Use the graph to find how much he must pay when he uses   (i)   60 units,   (ii)   104 units.

Errol uses x water units. This costs £c.
(b)   Use the information from the graph to find a formula for c in terms of x.   Edexcel

12 Water is poured at a constant rate into these containers.
Sketch the graphs of the depths of the water against time.

(a)

(b)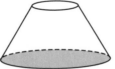

(c)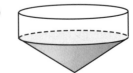

Simultaneous Equations

What you need to know

- A pair of **simultaneous equations** has the same unknown letters in each equation.

- To solve a pair of simultaneous equations find values for the unknown letters that fit **both** equations.

- Simultaneous equations can be solved either **graphically** or **algebraically**.

- Solving simultaneous equations **graphically** involves:
  - drawing the graphs of both equations,
  - finding the point where the graphs cross.

  When the graphs of both equations are parallel, the equations have no solution.

  Eg 1 Solve the simultaneous equations $x + 2y = 5$ and $x - 2y = 1$ graphically.

  For $x + 2y = 5$:
  When $x = 1$, $y = 2$.
  When $x = 5$, $y = 0$.
  Draw a line through the points
  $(1, 2)$ and $(5, 0)$.

  For $x - 2y = 1$:
  When $x = 1$, $y = 0$.
  When $x = 5$, $y = 2$.
  Draw a line through the points
  $(1, 0)$ and $(5, 2)$.

  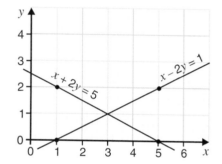

  The values of x and y at the point where the lines cross give the solution to the simultaneous equations.
  The lines cross at the point $(3, 1)$. This gives the solution $x = 3$ and $y = 1$.

- Solving simultaneous equations **algebraically** involves using either:
  - the **elimination** method, or
  - the **substitution** method.

  Eg 2 Solve the simultaneous equations $5x + 2y = 11$ and $3x - 4y = 4$ algebraically.

  $$5x + 2y = 11 \quad \text{A}$$
  $$3x - 4y = 4 \quad \text{B}$$

  | To make the number of y's the same we can multiply equation A by 2. |

  $\text{A} \times 2$ gives $\quad 10x + 4y = 22 \quad \text{C}$
  $$\phantom{\text{A} \times 2 \text{ gives} \quad} 3x - 4y = 4 \quad \text{D}$$

  $\text{C} + \text{D}$ gives $\quad\quad\quad 13x = 26$
  $$\phantom{\text{C} + \text{D} \text{ gives} \quad\quad\quad} x = 2$$

  | The number of y's is the **same** but the **signs** are **different**. To eliminate the y's the equations must be **added**. |

  Substitute $x = 2$ into $5x + 2y = 11$.
  $$10 + 2y = 11$$
  $$2y = 1$$
  $$y = 0.5$$

  | You can check the solution by substituting $x = 2$ and $y = 0.5$ into $3x - 4y = 4$. |

  The solution is $x = 2$ and $y = 0.5$.

- You should be able to find solutions to problems which involve forming and then solving simultaneous equations.

1 (a) On the same axes, draw the graphs of $y = 2x$ and $y = 6 - x$.
(b) Explain how you could use your graphs to solve the equation $2x = 6 - x$.

2 The diagram shows the graphs of the equations
$x + y = 1$ and $y = x - 5$.

Use the diagram to solve the simultaneous equations
$x + y = 1$ and $y = x - 5$.

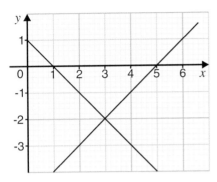

Edexcel

3 (a) On the same axes, draw the graphs of $y + x = 4$ and $y - 3x = 2$
for values of x from -2 to 2.
(b) Hence, solve the simultaneous equations $y + x = 4$ and $y - 3x = 2$.

4 Solve graphically the simultaneous equations $y = 3 - x$ and $y = x - 2$.

5 (a) On the same axes, draw the graphs of $x + y = 4$ and $y = x + 2$.
(b) Use the graphs to solve the simultaneous equations $x + y = 4$ and $y = x + 2$. Edexcel

6 The sketch shows the graph of $y = 2x - 1$.
Copy the diagram.

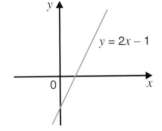

(a) On your diagram, sketch the graph of $y = 2x + 1$.
(b) Explain why the equations $y = 2x - 1$ and $y = 2x + 1$
cannot be solved simultaneously.

7 Solve these simultaneous equations. $6x + y = 7$
$2x - y = -3$

8 Solve the simultaneous equations $x + 3y = 13$ and $4x + 2y = 2$.

9 Solve the simultaneous equations. $3x + y = 13$
$2x - 3y = 16$
Edexcel

10 Heather sold 40 boxes of cards to raise money for charity.
She sold x small boxes at £4 each and y large boxes at £7 each.
She raised £184 altogether.
(a) Write down two equations connecting x and y.
(b) Solve these simultaneous equations to find how many of each size of box she sold.

11 Micro-scooters costs £x each and pogo sticks cost £y each.
2 micro-scooters and 4 pogo sticks cost £65.
1 micro-scooter and 3 pogo sticks cost £40.
(a) Write down two equations connecting x and y.
(b) Solve these simultaneous equations to find the cost of a micro-scooter and a pogo stick.

12 Solve these simultaneous equations. $2x + 5y = -1$ and $6x - y = 5$ Edexcel

13 Solve the simultaneous equations $2x + 3y = 7$ and $3x - 2y = 17$.

More or Less

● ● ● ● ● ● ● ● ● ● ● ● ●

What you need to know

- **Inequalities** can be described using words or numbers and symbols.

Sign	Meaning
$<$	is less than
$\leq$	is less than or equal to

Sign	Meaning
$>$	is greater than
$\geq$	is greater than or equal to

- Inequalities can be shown on a **number line**.

  Eg 1 This diagram shows the inequality: $-2 < x \leq 3$

  (number line from -3 to 4, open circle at -2, filled circle at 3)

  The circle is: **filled** if the inequality is **included** (i.e. $\leq$ or $\geq$),
  not filled if the inequality is **not included** (i.e. $<$ or $>$).

- **Solving inequalities** means finding the values of x which make the inequality true.

  The same rules for equations can be applied to inequalities, with one exception:
  When you **multiply** (or **divide**) both sides an inequality by a negative number the inequality is reversed. For example, if $-3x < 6$ then $x > -2$.

  Eg 2 Solve these inequalities.
  (a) $7a \geq a + 9$ (b) $-3x < 6$
  $\quad 6a \geq 9$ $\quad\ \ x > -2$
  $\quad\ \ a \geq 1.5$

  > Divide both sides by -3.
  > Because we are dividing by a negative number the inequality is reversed.

  Eg 3 Find the integer values of n for which $\ -1 \leq 2n + 3 < 7$.
  $$-1 \leq 2n + 3 < 7$$
  $$-4 \leq 2n < 4$$
  $$-2 \leq n < 2$$

  Integer values which satisfy the inequality $\ -1 \leq 2n + 3 < 7\ $ are: $\ -2, -1, 0, 1$

- Inequalities can be shown on a graph. A line divides the graph into two **regions**.

  To show an inequality on a graph: Replace the inequality by '=' and draw the line.
  For $>$ and $<$ the line is **broken**. For $\geq$ and $\leq$ the line is **solid**.
  Test a point on each side of the line to see whether its coordinates satisfy the inequality.
  Label the required region.

  Eg 4 Show the region which satisfies these inequalities:
  $y < 3$, $1 < x < 4$ and $2y > x$.

  (graph with lines $x = 1$, $x = 4$, $y = 3$, $2y = x$, shaded region)

  Eg 5 Use inequalities to describe the shaded region in this diagram.

  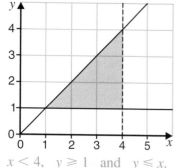

  $x < 4$, $y \geq 1$ and $y \leq x$.

1 Solve these inequalities.
(a) $5x > 15$ (b) $x + 3 \geqslant 1$ (c) $2x \leqslant 6 - x$ (d) $3 - 2x > 7$

2 Draw number lines to show each of these inequalities.
(a) $x \geqslant -2$ (b) $\frac{x}{3} < -1$ (c) $-1 < x \leqslant 3$ (d) $x \leqslant -1$ **and** $x > 3$

3 List all the possible integer values of n such that $-3 \leqslant n < 2$.   Edexcel

4 n is a whole number such that $6 < 2n < 13$. List all the possible values of n.   Edexcel

5 List the values of n, where n is an integer such that:
(a) $-2 \leqslant 2n < 6$ (b) $-3 < n - 3 \leqslant -1$ (c) $-5 \leqslant 2n - 3 < 1$

6 Solve the inequalities.   (a) $2x - 5 > x + 2$ (b) $-9 < 5x + 1 \leqslant 6$

7 Solve the inequality $7y > 2y - 3$.   Edexcel

8 Match each of the inequalities to its **unshaded** region.

    1 $x + y < 2$
    2 $y > 2$
    3 $y > x$
    4 $x < 2$

 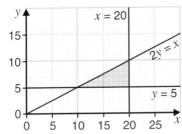 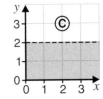 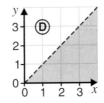

9 Draw and label axes for both x and y from 0 to 4.
(a) On your diagram draw and label the lines $y = 1$ and $x + y = 3$.
(b) Show clearly on the diagram the single region that is satisfied by all of these inequalities.
    $x \geqslant 0$, $y \geqslant 1$, $x + y \leqslant 3$. Label this region R.

10 Write down three inequalities which describe the shaded region.

11 (a) Draw and label axes for x from -1 to 4 and for y from 0 to 6.
    On your diagram draw and label the following lines. $y = 5$, $y = x + 1$ and $y = 6 - 2x$
(b) Show clearly the single region that is satisfied by **all** of these inequalities.
    $x \geqslant 0$, $y \leqslant 5$, $y \geqslant x + 1$, $y \leqslant 6 - 2x$.

12 Solve the following inequalities.   (a) $3 > x - 2$ (b) $3(x - 2) > 2(3 - x)$

13 (a) Solve the inequality $-4 \leqslant 2(x + 3) < 8$.
(b) n is an integer.
    Find the maximum value of n that satisfies the inequality $-4 \leqslant 2(x + 3) < 8$.

14 (a) Solve each of the following inequalities.   (i) $2x - 7 \leqslant 8 - x$ (ii) $3(2x + 1) > 15$
(b) Write down the whole number values of x which satisfy both of the above inequalities simultaneously.

Quadratic and Other Equations

What you need to know

- Brackets, such as $(x + 2)(x + 3)$, can be multiplied out using the **diagram method**, or by **expanding**.

  Eg 1 Multiply out $(x + 2)(x + 3)$.

  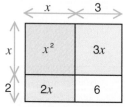

  $(x + 2)(x + 3) = x^2 + 3x + 2x + 6$
  $= x^2 + 5x + 6$

  Eg 2 Expand $(x - 3)(2x + 1)$.

  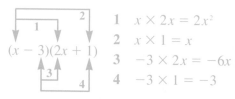

  1 $x \times 2x = 2x^2$
  2 $x \times 1 = x$
  3 $-3 \times 2x = -6x$
  4 $-3 \times 1 = -3$

  $(x - 3)(2x + 1) = 2x^2 + x - 6x - 3$
  $= 2x^2 - 5x - 3$

- **Factorising** is the opposite operation to removing brackets.

  Eg 3 Factorise the following.
  (a) $x^2 + 3x = x(x + 3)$
  (b) $x^2 - 25 = (x - 5)(x + 5)$
  (c) $x^2 + 3x - 10 = (x + 5)(x - 2)$

  > When factorising, work logically.
  > 1. Does the expression have a **common factor**?
  > 2. Is the expression a **difference of two squares**?
  > $a^2 - b^2 = (a - b)(a + b)$
  > 3. Will the expression factorise into **two brackets**?

- To write an algebraic fraction in its **simplest form**:
  factorise the numerator and denominator of the fraction,
  divide the numerator and denominator by their highest common factor.

  Eg 4 Simplify. (a) $\dfrac{5x - 10}{5} = \dfrac{5(x - 2)}{5} = x - 2$ (b) $\dfrac{2x - 4}{x^2 - 2x} = \dfrac{2(x - 2)}{x(x - 2)} = \dfrac{2}{x}$

- **Quadratic equations** can be solved by factorising.

  Eg 5 Solve these equations.
  (a) $x^2 - 5x = 0$
      $x(x - 5) = 0$
      $x = 0$ or 5
  (b) $a^2 - 4a + 3 = 0$
      $(a - 1)(a - 3) = 0$
      $a = 1$ or 3
  (c) $m^2 + m - 6 = 0$
      $(m - 2)(m + 3) = 0$
      $m = 2$ or -3

- **Quadratic equations** can be solved graphically.

  Eg 6 (a) Draw the graph of $y = x^2 - 2x - 5$ for values of x from -2 to 4.
  (b) Use your graph to solve the equation $x^2 - 2x - 5 = 0$.

  (a)
  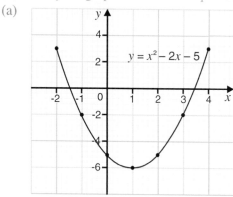

  > To draw a graph:
  > Make a table of values connecting x and y.
  > Plot the points.
  > Join the points with a smooth curve.

x	-2	-1	0	1	2	3	4
y	3	-2	-5	-6	-5	-2	3

  > To solve the equation, read the values of x where the graph of $y = x^2 - 2x - 5$ crosses the x axis ($y = 0$).

  (b) $x = -1.4$ and 3.4, correct to one decimal place.

- The general form for a **quadratic function** is
$y = ax^2 + bx + c$, where a cannot be zero.
The graph of a quadratic function is symmetrical
and has a **maximum** or **minimum** value.

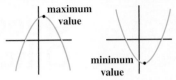

- The general form of a **cubic function** is $y = ax^3 + bx^2 + cx + d$, where a cannot be zero.
Cubic equations can be solved graphically or by trial and improvement.

- **Trial and improvement** is a method used to solve equations. The accuracy of the value of the
unknown letter is improved until the required degree of accuracy is obtained.

> **Eg 7** Use a trial and improvement method to find a solution to the equation $x^3 + x = 40$,
> correct to one decimal place.

x	$x^3 + x$	Comment
3	$27 + 3 = 30$	Too small
4	$64 + 4 = 68$	Too big
3.5	$42.8\ldots + 3.5 = 46.3\ldots$	Too big
3.3	$35.9\ldots + 3.3 = 39.2\ldots$	Too small
3.35	$37.5\ldots + 3.35 = 40.9\ldots$	Too big

For accuracy to 1 d.p.
check the second decimal place.
The solution lies between
3.3 and 3.35.

$x = 3.3$, correct to 1 d.p.

Exercise 19

1 Multiply out and simplify.
(a) $x(x - 7)$ (b) $(x - 2)(x + 5)$ (c) $(x + 3)(x - 5)$ (d) $(2x - 1)(x + 3)$

2 (a) Expand and simplify $4(x + 3) + 3(2x - 3)$.
(b) Expand and simplify $(2x - y)(3x + 4y)$. *Edexcel*

3 Expand and simplify $(3x + 2y)^2$.

4 Factorise.
(a) $x^2 - 6x$ (b) $x^2 + 6x + 9$ (c) $x^2 + 2x - 15$ (d) $x^2 - 4x + 3$

5 (a) Factorise $2x + 8y$.
(b) Factorise completely $3ac^2 - 6ac$.
(c) Factorise $x^2 - 9x + 18$. *Edexcel*

6 Factorise $x^2 - 9$.

7 Simplify. (a) $\dfrac{3a + 12}{3}$ (b) $\dfrac{x^2 - 3x}{x}$ (c) $\dfrac{x^2 + 2x}{5x + 10}$ (d) $\dfrac{2x^2 - 6x}{4x - 12}$

8 Solve these equations.
(a) $x(x + 5) = 0$ (b) $(x - 3)(x + 2) = 0$ (c) $(2x + 3)(x - 1) = 0$

9 (a) Expand and simplify $(2x - 5)(x + 3)$.
(b) (i) Factorise $x^2 + 6x - 7$. (ii) Solve the equation $x^2 + 6x - 7 = 0$. *Edexcel*

10 (a) Factorise $5x^2 - 10x$.
(b) Hence solve the equation $5x^2 - 10x = 0$.

11 Solve these equations.
(a) $x^2 - 3x = 0$ (b) $x^2 - 3x + 2 = 0$ (c) $x^2 - x - 6 = 0$

12 Solve by factorisation $x^2 + 4x - 5 = 0$.

13 Solve the equation $x^2 - 11x + 28 = 0$.

14 (a) Factorise $2x^2 - 5x - 3 = 0$.
  (b) Hence solve the equation $2x^2 - 5x - 3 = 0$.

15 Solve the equation $2x^2 + x - 1 = 0$.

16 Match these equations to their graphs.

  1 $y = 1 - x^2$
  2 $y = x^3$
  3 $y = x^2 - 1$
  4 $y = 1 - 2x$

A

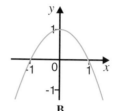
B

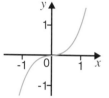
C

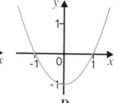
D

17 (a) Copy and complete the table of values for $y = 2x^2$.

x	-3	-2	-1	0	1	2	3
y	18				2	8	

  (b) Draw the graph of $y = 2x^2$.
  (c) Use your graph to find (i) the value of y when $x = 2.5$,
    (ii) the values of x when $y = 12$.

  Edexcel

18 (a) Draw the graph for $y = 5 - x^2$ for values of x from -3 to 3.
  (b) State the maximum value of y.
  (c) Use your graph to solve the equation $5 - x^2 = 0$.

19 (a) Copy and complete the table of values for $y = 2x^2 - 3x + 2$.

x	-2	-1	0	1	2	3
y	16		2		4	

  (b) Draw the graph of $y = 2x^2 - 3x + 2$ for values of x from -2 to 3.
  (c) Explain how the graph shows that there are no values of x for which $2x^2 - 3x + 2 = 0$.
  (d) State the minimum value of y.

20 (a) Draw the graph of $y = x^3 - x$ for $-3 \leqslant x \leqslant 3$.
  (b) Use your graph to find the value of x when $y = 10$.
  (c) Use your graph to solve the equation $x^3 - x = 0$.

21 Draw the graph of $y = \frac{1}{x}$ for values of x from -4 to 4.

22 In the diagram each side of the square $ABCD$
  is $(3 + x)$ cm.
  (a) Write down an expression in terms of x
    for the area, in cm^2, of the square $ABCD$.

  The actual area of the square $ABCD$ is 10 cm^2.
  (b) Show that $x^2 + 6x = 1$.

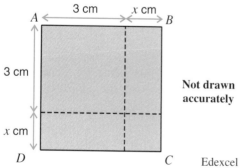

Not drawn accurately

  Edexcel

23 The equation $x^3 - 5x = 38$ has a solution between 3 and 4.
  Use a trial and improvement method to find this solution.
  Give your answer correct to 1 decimal place.
  You must shall **all** your working.

  Edexcel

Section Review - Algebra

1 Simplify (a) $7x - 5x + 3x$, (b) $a - 3b + 2a - b$, (c) $3 \times m \times m$.

2 (a) Find the value of $6a + 3b + c$ when $a = 1$, $b = 2$ and $c = 3$.

(b) Find the value of $\dfrac{3(m + 9)}{n}$ when $m = -5$ and $n = 24$.

(c) Find the value of $3p + q$ when $p = -2$ and $q = 5$.

3 (a) On graph paper, plot the points $A(-3, -2)$ and $B(1, 4)$.
(b) What are the coordinates of the midpoint of AB?

4 A jam doughnut costs t pence.
(a) Write an expression for the cost of 5 jam doughnuts.

A cream doughnut costs 5 pence more than a jam doughnut.
(b) Write an expression for the cost of a cream doughnut.

5 Solve (a) $x - 3 = 7$, (b) $3x = 6$, (c) $5x + 4 = 19$.

6 Nick thinks of a number.
He doubles it and then subtracts 3. The answer is 17. What is his number?

7 (a) What is the next term in this sequence? 2, 9, 16, 23, …
(b) Will the 50th term in the sequence be an odd number or an even number?
Give a reason for your answer.

8 (a) Simplify (i) $x + x + x$ (ii) $2a + 4b + a - 2b$ (iii) $3(a + 2)$
(b) Expand and simplify $2(x - 1) + 3(2x + 1)$ Edexcel

9 Here is an input-output diagram.

Input ⟶ | multiply by −2 | ⟶ | subtract 3 | ⟶ Output

(a) What is the output when the input is -5?
(b) What is the input when the output is -5?

10 Here are the first five numbers in a simple number sequence.

$$1, \quad 3, \quad 7, \quad 13, \quad 21, \quad …$$

(a) Write down the next two numbers in the sequence.
(b) Describe, in words, the rule to continue this sequence.   Edexcel

11 (a) Copy and complete the table of values for $y = 3x - 2$.

x	-1	0	1	2	3
$y = 3x - 2$					

(b) Plot your values for x and y. Join your points with a straight line.
(c) Write down the coordinates of the point where your graph crosses the y axis.   Edexcel

12 Solve (a) $x + 7 = 4$, (b) $4x = 10$, (c) $2x + 5 = 11$.

13 Choc Bars cost 27 pence each.
Write down a formula for the cost, C pence, of n Choc Bars.   Edexcel

14 John uses this rule:

Think of a number, subtract 3 and then double the result.

John's answer is 8.
What number did he start with?

48

15 Hannah is x years old.
  (a) Her sister Louisa is 3 years younger than Hannah.
      Write an expression, in terms of x, for Louisa's age.
  (b) Their mother is four times as old as Hannah.
      Write an expression, in terms of x, for their mother's age.
  (c) The total of their ages is 45 years.
      By forming an equation in x, find their ages.

16 (a) Solve the equations   (i) $4(a - 2) = 6$,   (ii) $5t + 3 = -1 + t$.
  (b) The sum of the numbers x, $x - 3$ and $x + 7$ is 25.
      By forming an equation in x, find the value of x.

17 (a) Solve $4p + 6 = 26$.
  (b) Solve $5(2q + 6) = 25$.
  (c) Solve $18y - 27 = 10y - 25$.   *Edexcel*

18 Sharon earns b pounds an hour.
She worked for h hours.
She also earned a bonus of c pounds.
Write down a formula for her total earnings, P pounds.   *Edexcel*

19 Here is a rule to change kilograms to pounds.

> Multiply the number of kilograms by 22 and then divide by 10.

  (a) Use the rule to change 5 kilograms to pounds.
  (b) Write a formula to change K kilograms to L pounds.
  (c) Use your formula to find the value of K when $L = 55$.

20 (a) Factorise   (i) $3a - 6$,   (ii) $k^2 - 2k$.
  (b) Multiply out (i) $5(x + 3)$,   (ii) $m(m - 4)$.
  (c) Solve   (i) $3 - 4x = x + 8$,   (ii) $3(2x + 1) = 6$.

21 (a) On the same diagram draw the graphs $2y = x + 4$ and $y = \frac{1}{2}x + 1$.
  (b) What do you notice about the two lines you have drawn?

22 Solve the equation $\dfrac{3x - 5}{8} = 5$.   *Edexcel*

23 A sequence begins 1, −1, …
This rule is used to continue the sequence.

> Multiply the last number by 2 and then subtract 3.

  (a) What is the next term in the sequence?
  (b) A term in the sequence is called x.
      Write, in terms of x, the next term in the sequence.

24 (a) Copy and complete the table of values for $y = x^2 - 3$.

x	-2	-1	0	1	2	3
y		-2	-3			6

  (b) Draw the graph of $y = x^2 - 3$ for values of x from -2 to 3.
  (c) Use your graph to solve the equation $x^2 - 3 = 0$.

25 Here are the first five numbers of a simple number sequence.

$$1, \quad 5, \quad 9, \quad 13, \quad 17, \quad \ldots$$

  (a) Write down the next two numbers in the sequence.
  (b) Describe, in words, the rule to continue this sequence.
  (c) Write down, in terms of n, the nth term in this sequence.   *Edexcel*

26 A solution of the equation $x^3 - 9x = 5$ is between 3 and 4.
Use the method of trial and improvement to find this solution.
Give your answer correct to 2 decimal places. You must show **all** your working. Edexcel

27

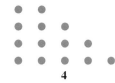

| Pattern Number | 1 | 2 | 3 | 4 |

The diagrams show patterns made of dots.
The number of dots in each pattern is shown in the table below.

Pattern number	1	2	3	4	5	6
Number of dots	2	5	9	14		

(a) Copy and complete the table.
(b) (i) Work out the number of dots in pattern number 10.
    (ii) Give a reason for your answer.

The first 4 triangular numbers are: 1, 3, 6, 10.

An expression for the nth triangular number is $\dfrac{n(n+1)}{2}$.

(c) Use this to write down an expression for the number of dots in pattern number n.
(d) Work out the number of dots in pattern number 99. Edexcel

28 (a) Solve the inequality $3x < 6 - x$.
(b) List all the values of n, where n is an integer, such that $-3 < 2x + 1 \leqslant 3$.

29 Match these equations to their graphs.

A $y = x$
B $y + x = 1$
C $y = x^2$
D $y = x^3$

P   Q   R   S

30 The volume, V, of the barrel is given by the formula:
$$V = \frac{\pi H (2R^2 + r^2)}{3000}$$

$\pi = 3.14$, $H = 60$, $R = 25$ and $r = 20$.

Calculate the value of V.
Give your answer correct to 3 significant figures.

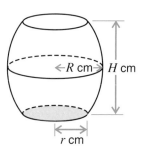
$\leftarrow R$ cm $\quad H$ cm
r cm
Edexcel

31 Make x the subject of the formula $y = 2x - 5$.

32

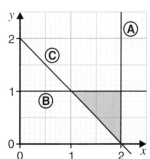

(a) Write down the equations of the lines labelled **A**, **B** and **C** in the diagram.

(b) Write down three inequalities to describe the shaded region.

33 (a) Draw the graph of $y = x^2 - 2x + 1$ for values of x from -1 to 3.
(b) Use your graph to solve the equation $x^2 - 2x + 1 = 0$.
(c) Use your graph to solve the equation $x^2 - 2x + 1 = 2$.

34 (a) Work out the value of $x^2 - 5x + 6$ when $x = -2$.
(b) (i) Factorise $x^2 - 5x + 6$.
(ii) Hence solve the equation $x^2 - 5x + 6 = 0$.

35 (a) Factorise (i) $2st - 4t$, (ii) $3y^2 + 6y$, (iii) $d^2 - 2d - 24$.
(b) Solve the equations (i) $x(x + 2) = 0$, (ii) $y^2 - 3y + 2 = 0$.
(c) Expand and simplify $(2x - 3)(x + 2)$.

36 $v = u - ft$
(a) Express t in terms of u, v and f.
(b) When $u = 10$ and $v = 2$, write down the formula for t in terms of f.
(c) Given that $1 \leqslant f \leqslant 10$, and that t is a **whole number**, use your answer to (b) to write down all the possible values of t.

Edexcel

37 The line with equation $3y = -2x + 6$ has been drawn on the grid.
(a) Copy the diagram and draw the graph of $y = 2x - 2$ on the same grid.
(b) Use the graphs to find the solution of the simultaneous equations $3y = -2x + 6$ and $y = 2x - 2$.
A line is drawn parallel to $3y = -2x + 6$ through the point $(2, 1)$.
(c) Find the equation of this line.

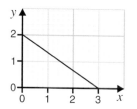

Edexcel

38 (a) Expand $x(x + 4)$.
(b) Solve the simultaneous equations $x + 8y = 5$ and $3x - 4y = 8$.

Edexcel

39 (a) Simplify. (i) $\dfrac{p^6}{p^2}$ (ii) $q^3 \times q$ (iii) $(x^3)^2$
(b) Factorise completely $9x^2y - 6xy^3$.

Edexcel

40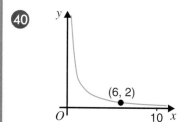

The graph of a function has been sketched for $0 < x \leqslant 10$.
The equation of the function is **one** of the following:

$$y = kx^3 \quad \textbf{or} \quad y = kx^2 \quad \textbf{or} \quad y = \frac{k}{x}$$

where k is a positive constant.
By choosing the appropriate equation and using the point $(6, 2)$ which lies on the curve, calculate the value of k.

Edexcel

41 (a) The graph of a straight line is shown.
What is the equation of the line?

(b) The equation of a different line is $4y - 3x = 8$.
What is the gradient of this line?

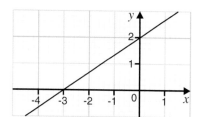

42 (a) Simplify $\dfrac{x^2 - 3x}{3x - 9}$. (b) Factorise fully $3x^2 - 12$. (c) Solve $x^2 + 3x - 10 = 0$.

43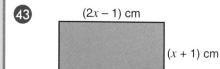

(2x − 1) cm

(x + 1) cm

The dimensions of a rectangle are shown.
The rectangle has an area of $104 \, \text{cm}^2$.
Form an equation for the area of the rectangle and show that it can be written in the form $2x^2 + x - 105 = 0$.

Angles

What you need to know

- Types and names of angles.

Acute angle	**Right angle**	**Obtuse angle**	**Reflex angle**

$0° < a < 90°$	$a = 90°$	$90° < a < 180°$	$180° < a < 360°$

- Angle properties.

Angles at a point	**Complementary angles**	**Supplementary angles**	**Vertically opposite angles**
		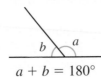	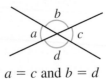
$a + b + c = 360°$	$x + y = 90°$	$a + b = 180°$	$a = c$ and $b = d$

- Lines which meet at right angles are **perpendicular** to each other.
- A straight line joining two points is called a **line segment**.
- Lines which never meet and are always the same distance apart are **parallel**.
- When two parallel lines are crossed by a **transversal** the following pairs of angles are formed.

Corresponding angles	**Alternate angles**	**Allied angles**	
			Arrowheads are used to show that lines are **parallel**.
$a = c$	$b = c$	$b + d = 180°$	

- You should be able to use angle properties to solve problems involving lines and angles.
- **Bearings** are used to describe the direction in which you must travel to get from one place to another.
- A bearing is an angle measured from the North line in a clockwise direction.
  A bearing can be any angle from $0°$ to $360°$ and is written as a three-figure number.

To find a bearing:
    measure angle a to find the bearing of Y from X,
    measure angle b to find the bearing of X from Y.

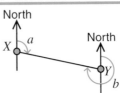

- Be able to use **scales** and **bearings** to interpret and draw accurate diagrams.

There are two ways to describe a scale.
1. A scale of 1 cm to 10 km means that a distance of 1 cm on the map represents an actual distance of 10 km.
2. A scale of 1 : 10 000 means that all distances measured on the map have to be multiplied by 10 000 to find the real distance.

1 Find the size of the lettered angles. Give a reason for each answer.

(a)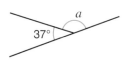

(b)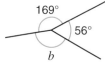

(c)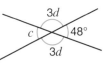

2 (a) (i) Work out the size of angle *p*.
(ii) Give a reason for your answer.

(b) (i) Work out the size of angle *q*.
(ii) Give a reason for your answer.

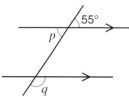

Edexcel

3 In the diagram, the lines *PQ* and *RS* are parallel.

(a) What is the size of angle *PQR*?
Give a reason for your answer.

(b) Find the size of angle *RQS*.

4 Find the size of the angles marked with letters.

(a)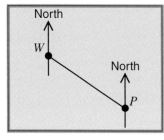

(b)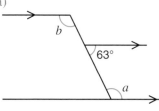

(c)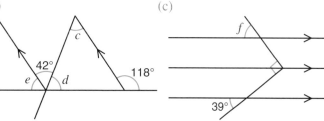

5 The dot represents a lighthouse.
The cross represents a ship.

Measure the 3-figure bearing
of the ship from the lighthouse.

Edexcel

6 The map shows the positions of a windmill, *W*, and a pylon, *P*.
(a) What is the bearing of
(i) the pylon from the windmill,
(ii) the windmill from the pylon?

The map has been drawn to a scale of 2 cm to 5 km.
(b) Use the map to find the distance *WP* in kilometres.

7 The diagram shows a sketch of the course to be
used for a running event.

(a) Draw an accurate plan of the course, using a
scale of 1 cm to represent 100 m.

(b) Use your plan to find
(i) the bearing of *X* from *Y*,
(ii) the distance *XY* in metres.

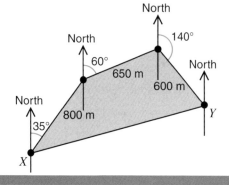

What you need to know

- A **triangle** is a shape made by three straight sides.

- Triangles can be: **acute-angled** (all angles less than 90°),
  obtuse-angled (one angle greater than 90°),
  right-angled (one angle equal to 90°).

- The sum of the angles in a triangle is 180°.
  $$a + b + c = 180°$$

- The exterior angle is equal to the sum of the two opposite interior angles. $a + b = d$

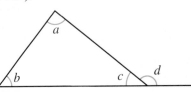

- Types of triangle:

  Scalene   **Isosceles**   **Equilateral**

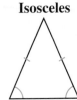

> A **sketch** is used when an accurate drawing is not required. Dashes across lines show sides that are equal in length. Equal angles are marked using arcs.

- You should be able to use properties of triangles to solve problems.

  Eg 1 Find the size of the angles marked a and b.
  $$a = 86° + 51° \quad (\text{ext. } \angle \text{ of a } \Delta)$$
  $$a = 137°$$
  $$b + 137° = 180° \quad (\text{supp. } \angle\text{'s})$$
  $$b = 43°$$

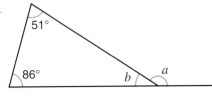

- Perimeter of a triangle is the sum of its three sides.

- Area of a triangle $= \dfrac{\text{base} \times \text{perpendicular height}}{2}$
  $$A = \tfrac{1}{2} \times b \times h$$

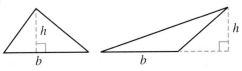

  Eg 2 Calculate the area of this triangle.
  $$A = \tfrac{1}{2} \times b \times h$$
  $$= \tfrac{1}{2} \times 9 \times 6 \, \text{cm}^2$$
  $$= 27 \, \text{cm}^2$$

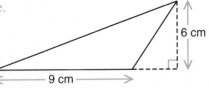

- You should be able to draw triangles accurately, using ruler, compasses and protractor.

Exercise 21

1 Without measuring, work out the size of the angles marked with letters.

(a)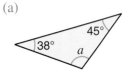

(b)

(c)

2 *ABC* and *EBD* are straight lines.
BD = *BC*.   Angle *CBD* = 42°.

(a) Write down the size of the angle marked *e*°.

(b) Work out the size of the angle marked *f*°.

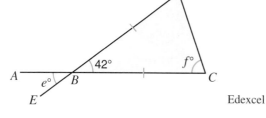

Edexcel

3

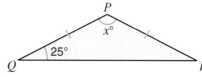

The diagram shows triangle *PQR*, with *PQ* = *PR*.
Work out the value of *x*.
Give a reason for your answer.

4 (a) (i) Write down the size of the angle marked *x*°.
  (ii) Give a reason for your answer.

(b) (i) Work out the size of the angle marked *y*°.
  (ii) Give a reason for your answer.

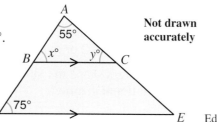

Not drawn accurately

Edexcel

5

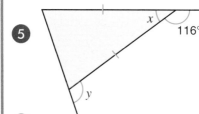

The diagram shows an isosceles triangle with two sides extended.

(a) Work out the size of angle *x*.

(b) Work out the size of angle *y*.

6 Make accurate drawings of these triangles using the information given.

(a)

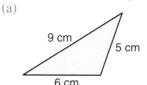

(b)

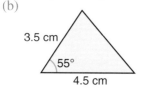

(c)

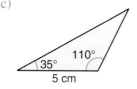

7 Find the areas of these triangles.

(a)

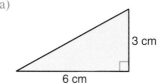

(b)

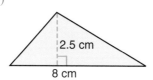

(c)

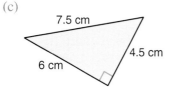

8 (a) Construct accurately a triangle with sides of 8 cm, 6 cm and 5 cm.
(b) By measuring the base and height, calculate the area of the triangle.

9 The diagram shows triangle *ABC*.
Calculate the area of triangle *ABC*.

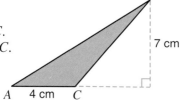

10

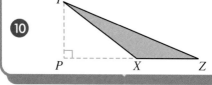

Triangle *XYZ* has an area of 12 cm². *XZ* = 5 cm.
Calculate *YP*.

Symmetry and Congruence

What you need to know

- A two-dimensional shape has **line symmetry** if the line divides the shape so that one side fits exactly over the other.

- A two-dimensional shape has **rotational symmetry** if it fits into a copy of its outline as it is rotated through 360°.

- A shape is only described as having rotational symmetry if the order of rotational symmetry is 2 or more.

- The number of times a shape fits into its outline in a single turn is the **order of rotational symmetry**.

Order of
rotational
symmetry 5

Eg 1 For each of these shapes (a) draw and state the number of lines of symmetry,
(b) state the order of rotational symmetry.

(i)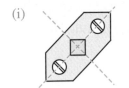

Two lines of symmetry.
Rotational symmetry of order 2.

(ii)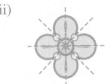

4 lines of symmetry.
Order of rotational symmetry 4.

(iii)

No lines of symmetry.
Order of rotational symmetry 1.
The shape is **not** described as
having rotational symmetry.

- A **plane of symmetry** slices through a three-dimensional object so that one half is the mirror image of the other half.

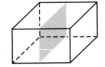

- Three-dimensional objects can have **axes of symmetry**.

Eg 2 Sketch a cuboid and show its axes of symmetry.

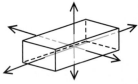

A cuboid has three axes of symmetry.
The order of rotational symmetry
about each axis is 2.

- When two shapes are the same shape and size they are said to be **congruent**.

- There are four ways to show that a pair of triangles are congruent.

SSS	3 corresponding sides.	**ASA**	2 angles and a corresponding side.
SAS	2 sides and the included angle.	**RHS**	Right angle, hypotenuse and one other side.

Eg 3 Which of these triangles are congruent to each other? Give a reason for your answer.

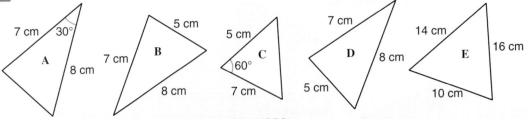

B and D.   Reason: 3 corresponding sides (SSS)

1 Half of a shape is drawn on squared paper, as shown. *AB* is a line of symmetry for the complete shape. Copy the diagram and complete the shape.

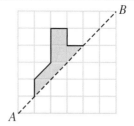

2 Consider the letters of the word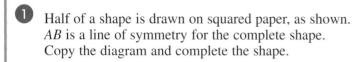

Which letters have (a) line symmetry only,
(b) rotational symmetry only,
(c) line symmetry and rotational symmetry?

3 For each of these shapes state (i) the number of lines of symmetry,
(ii) the order of rotational symmetry.

(a) (b) 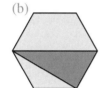 (c) 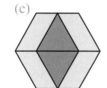 (d) 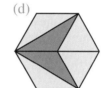 (e)

4 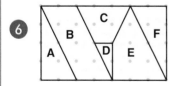 The diagram shows a square grid with two squares shaded.
Copy the diagram and shade two more squares so that the final diagram has rotational symmetry of order 2.

5 The diagram represents a prism.

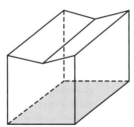

Copy the diagram and draw in one plane of symmetry on your diagram.

Edexcel

6 The diagram shows a rectangle which has been cut into 6 pieces. Which two pieces are congruent to each other?

7 The diagram shows information about four triangles.
Which two triangles are congruent?
Give a reason for your answer.

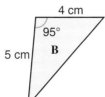 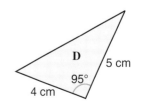

Quadrilaterals ●●●●●●●●●

What you need to know

- A **quadrilateral** is a shape made by four straight lines.

- The sum of the angles in a quadrilateral is 360°.

- The **perimeter** of a quadrilateral is the sum of the lengths of its four sides.

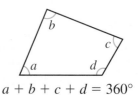

$$a + b + c + d = 360°$$

- Facts about these special quadrilaterals:

| parallelogram | rectangle | square | rhombus | trapezium | isosceles trapezium | kite |

Quadrilateral	Sides	Angles	Diagonals	Line symmetry	Order of rotational symmetry	Area formula
Parallelogram	Opposite sides equal and parallel	Opposite angles equal	Bisect each other	0	2	$A = bh$
Rectangle	Opposite sides equal and parallel	All 90°	Bisect each other	2	2	$A = bh$
Rhombus	4 equal sides, opposite sides parallel	Opposite angles equal	Bisect each other at 90°	2	2	$A = bh$
Square	4 equal sides, opposite sides parallel	All 90°	Bisect each other at 90°	4	4	$A = l^2$
Trapezium	1 pair of parallel sides					$A = \frac{1}{2}(a + b)h$
Isosceles trapezium	1 pair of parallel sides, non-parallel sides equal	2 pairs of equal angles	Equal in length	1	1*	$A = \frac{1}{2}(a + b)h$
Kite	2 pairs of adjacent sides equal	1 pair of opposite angles equal	One bisects the other at 90°	1	1*	

*A shape is only described as having rotational symmetry if the order of rotational symmetry is 2 or more.

- You should be able to use properties of quadrilaterals to solve problems.

Eg 1 Work out the size of the angle marked x.

Opposite angles are equal.
So, $125° + 125° + x + x = 360°$
$x = 55°$

Eg 2 Find the area of this trapezium.
$A = \frac{1}{2}(a + b)h$
$= \frac{1}{2}(6 + 9)5$
$= \frac{1}{2} \times 15 \times 5$
$= 37.5 \text{ cm}^2$

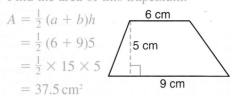

- You should be able to construct a quadrilateral from given information using ruler, protractor, compasses.

1 (a) Name each quadrilateral which has all its sides of equal length.
(b) Name each quadrilateral which has only one pair of parallel sides.
(c) Name each quadrilateral which has two pairs of parallel sides, but no angles of 90° between its sides.

Edexcel

2 Find the size of the lettered angles.

(a) 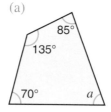   (b)   (c)   (d)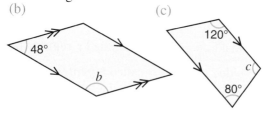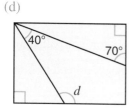

3 (a) (i) Work out the value of x.
(ii) Give a reason for your answer.

(b) (i) Work out the value of y.
(ii) Give a reason for your answer.

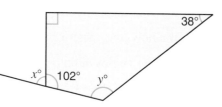

Edexcel

4 The diagram shows a quadrilateral $ABCD$.
$AB = BC$ and $CD = DA$.
(a) Which of the following correctly describes the quadrilateral $ABCD$?
rhombus   **parallelogram**   **kite**   **trapezium**

(b) Angle $ADC = 36°$ and angle $BCD = 105°$.
Work out the size of angle ABC.

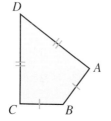

5 $ABCD$ is a quadrilateral.
$AB = 6$ cm, $AC = 9$ cm, $BC = 5$ cm, $AD = 3.5$ cm and angle $BAD = 66°$.
Make an accurate drawing of the quadrilateral $ABCD$.

Edexcel

6 Work out the area of
(a) the square $EBCD$,
(b) the triangle ABE.

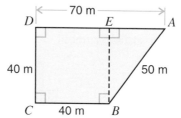

Edexcel

7 A rectangle measures 8.6 cm by 6.4 cm.
(a) Find the perimeter of the rectangle.
(b) Find the area of the rectangle.

8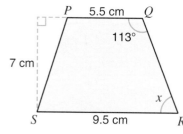

The diagram shows a trapezium $PQRS$.
(a) Work out the size of the angle marked x.
(b) Calculate the area of the trapezium.

9 A rectangular carpet is twice as long as it is wide.
The carpet covers an area of 24.5 m².
Calculate the length of the carpet.

Polygons

What you need to know

- A **polygon** is a many-sided shape made by straight lines.

- A polygon with all sides equal and all angles equal is called a **regular polygon**.

- Shapes you need to know: A 5-sided polygon is called a **pentagon**.
  A 6-sided polygon is called a **hexagon**.
  An 8-sided polygon is called an **octagon**.

- The sum of the exterior angles of any polygon is 360°.

- At each vertex of a polygon: interior angle + exterior angle = 180°

- The sum of the interior angles of an n-sided polygon is given by:
  $(n - 2) \times 180°$

- For a regular n-sided polygon: exterior angle = $\dfrac{360°}{n}$

interior angle
exterior angle

- You should be able to use the properties of polygons to solve problems.

  Eg 1   To find the sum of the interior angles of a pentagon substitute $n = 5$ into $(n - 2) \times 180°$.
  $(5 - 2) \times 180° = 3 \times 180° = 540°$

  Eg 2   A regular polygon has an exterior angle of 30°.
  (a)   How many sides has the polygon?
  (b)   What is the size of an interior angle of the polygon?

  (a) $n = \dfrac{360°}{\text{exterior angle}}$ (b)   int. $\angle$ + ext. $\angle$ = 180°
  $n = \frac{360°}{30°}$ int. $\angle$ + 30° = 180°
  $n = 12$ interior angle = 150°

- A shape will **tessellate** if it covers a surface without overlapping and leaves no gaps.

- All triangles tessellate.

- All quadrilaterals tessellate.

- Equilateral triangles, squares and hexagons can be used to make **regular tessellations**.

- A regular pentagon cannot be used to make a regular tessellation.

Exercise 24

1. Work out the size of the angles marked with letters.

   (a)

   (b)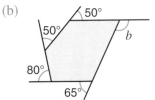

   (c)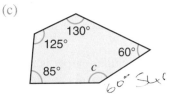

2 These shapes are regular polygons.
Work out the size of the lettered angles.

(a)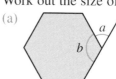

(b)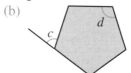

(c)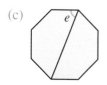

3 *ABCDEF* is a regular hexagon with centre *O*.
(a) What type of triangle is *ABO*?
(b) (i) Work out the size of the angle marked *x*°.
 (ii) Work out the size of the angle marked *y*°.
(c) (i) What type of quadrilateral is *BCDO*?
 (ii) Draw a diagram to show how three such
 quadrilaterals can tessellate to make a hexagon.

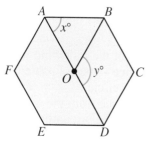

Edexcel

4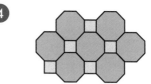

(a) Here is a pattern of regular octagons and squares.
Explain why these shapes tessellate.

(b) Draw a tessellation which uses equilateral triangles and
regular hexagons.

5 Four regular pentagons are placed together, as shown,
to form a rhombus, *ABCD*.

Calculate the size of
(a) angle *ABC*,
(b) angle *XCY*.

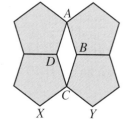

6 Each diagram shows part of a regular polygon.
How many sides has each polygon?

(a)

(b)

7 (a) A regular polygon has 9 sides.
Find the size of an interior angle.
(b) A regular polygon has an exterior angle of 20°.
Show that the sum of the interior angles is 2880°.

8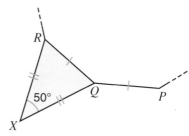

PQ and *QR* are two sides of a regular 10-sided polygon.
QRX is an isosceles triangle with *RX* = *XQ*.
Angle *QXR* = 50°.

Work out the size of the obtuse angle *PQX*.

9 The diagram shows part of an inscribed regular polygon.
The line *AB* is one side of the polygon.
O is the centre of the circle.
Angle *AOB* = 30°.

Show that the polygon has 12 sides and hence find the sum of its interior angles.

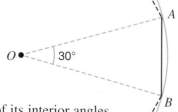

Circle Properties

What you need to know

- A **circle** is the shape drawn by keeping a pencil the same distance from a fixed point on a piece of paper.

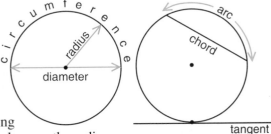

- The meaning of the following words:
  Circumference – special name used for the perimeter of a circle.
  Radius – distance from the centre of the circle to any point on the circumference.
  The plural of radius is **radii**.
  Diameter – distance right across the circle, passing through the centre point. The diameter is twice as long as the radius.
  Chord – a line joining two points on the circumference. The longest chord is the diameter.
  Tangent – a line which touches the circumference of a circle at one point only.
  Arc – part of the circumference of a circle.
  Segment – a chord divides a circle into two segments.
  Sector – two radii divide a circle into two sectors.

- The vertices of a **cyclic quadrilateral** lie on the circumference of a circle.

- **Circle properties**

 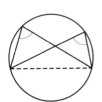 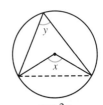

The angle in a semi-circle is a right angle.

Angles in the same segment are equal.

$x = 2y$
The angle at the centre is twice the angle at the circumference.

$p + r = 180°$ and $q + s = 180°$
Opposite angles of a cyclic quadrilateral are supplementary.

- A tangent is perpendicular to the radius at the point of contact.

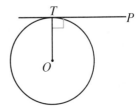

- Tangents drawn to a circle from the same point are equal in length.

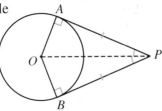

- You should be able to use circle properties to solve problems.

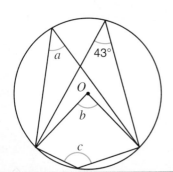

  Eg 1 O is the centre of the circle. Find the marked angles.
  $a = 43°$ (angles in the same segment)
  $b = 2 × 43°$ ($\angle$ at centre = twice $\angle$ at circum.)
  $b = 86°$
  $c = 180° - 43°$ (opp. $\angle$s of a cyclic quad)
  $c = 137°$

The diagrams in this exercise have not been drawn accurately.

1 *O* is the centre of the circle.
Work out the size of the lettered angles. Give a reason for each of your answers.

(a)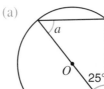

(b)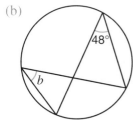

(c)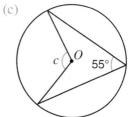

(d)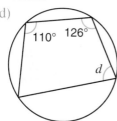

2 Look at the diagram.
Find angles *a* and *d*, when   *b* = 48°   and   *c* = 32°.

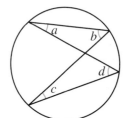

3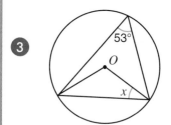

O is the centre of the circle.
Work out the size of angle *x*.

4 *AB* is a tangent to the circle centre *O*.
Angle *OAB* = 28°.
Find the size of angle *BCO*.

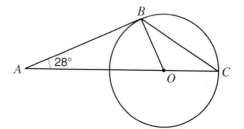

5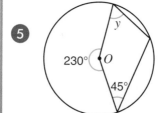

O is the centre of the circle.
Work out the size of angle *y*.

6 *AXB* is a tangent to the circle, centre *O*.
Find the size of the angles marked *a*, *b* and *c*.

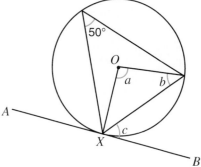

7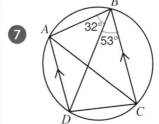

ABCD is a cyclic quadrilateral.
AD is parallel to *BC*.   ∠*ABD* = 32°   and   ∠*CBD* = 53°.
Find   (a)   angle *ADB*,   (b)   angle *ACD*,
         (c)   angle *ADC*,   (d)   angle *BAD*.

8 The diagram shows a semi-circle, centre *O*.
Angle *CAD* = *x*°   and   *BC* is parallel to *AD*.
Find, in terms of *x*, angle *ABC*.

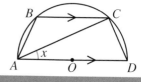

Circles and Other Shapes

What you need to know

- The meaning of the words radius, diameter, circumference.

- The **circumference** of a circle is given by:

$$C = \pi \times d \quad \text{or} \quad C = 2 \times \pi \times r$$

- The **area** of a circle is given by:

$$A = \pi \times r^2$$

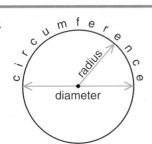

diameter = 2 × radius

- You should be able to solve problems which involve finding the circumference or the area of a circle.

In all calculations take π to be 3.14 or use the π key on your calculator.

Eg 1 Find the circumference of a circle with radius 9 cm.
Give your answer to 1 d.p.

$C = 2 \times \pi \times r$
$\quad = 2 \times \pi \times 9$
$\quad = 56.548\ldots$
$\quad = 56.5\,\text{cm}$, correct to 1 d.p.

Eg 2 Find the area of a circle with radius 6 cm.
Give your answer to 3 sig. figs.

$A = \pi \times r^2$
$\quad = \pi \times 6 \times 6$
$\quad = 113.097\ldots$
$\quad = 113\,\text{cm}^2$, correct to 3 sig. figs.

Eg 3 A circle has a circumference of 25.2 cm.
Find the diameter of the circle.

$C = \pi d \quad \text{so} \quad d = \dfrac{C}{\pi}$

$d = \dfrac{25.2}{\pi}$

$\quad = 8.021\ldots$

$\quad = 8.0\,\text{cm}$, correct to 1 d.p.

Eg 4 A circle has an area of 154 cm².
Find the radius of the circle.

$A = \pi r^2 \quad \text{so} \quad r^2 = \dfrac{A}{\pi}$

$r^2 = \dfrac{154}{\pi} = 49.019\ldots$

$r = \sqrt{49.019\ldots} = 7.001\ldots$

$r = 7\,\text{cm}$, to the nearest cm.

- Shapes formed by joining different shapes together are called **compound shapes**.
To find the area of a compound shape we must first divide the shape up into rectangles, triangles, circles, etc, and find the area of each part.

Eg 5 Find the area of this metal plate.

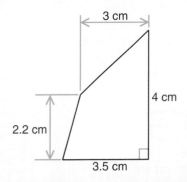

The plate can be split into a rectangle, A, and two triangles, B and C.

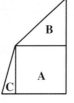

Area $A = 3 \times 2.2 = 6.6\,\text{cm}^2$

Area $B = \dfrac{3 \times 1.8}{2} = 2.7\,\text{cm}^2$

Area $C = \dfrac{0.5 \times 2.2}{2} = 0.55\,\text{cm}^2$

Total area $= 6.6 + 2.7 + 0.55 = 9.85\,\text{cm}^2$

Take π to be 3.14 or use the π key on your calculator.
Do not use a calculator for questions 1 and 2.

1 A circular pond has a diameter of 19.8 metres.
(a) **Estimate** the circumference of the pond.
(b) **Estimate** the area of the pond.

2 This diagram shows the plan of a floor.

(a) Work out the perimeter of the floor.

(b) Work out the area of the floor.

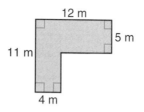

Edexcel

3 The radius of a circle is 5.1 m.
Work out the area of the circle.

Edexcel

4 Tranter has completed three-fifths of a circular jigsaw puzzle.
The puzzle has a radius of 20 cm.
What area of the puzzle is complete?

5 The diagram shows a circle of diameter 70 cm
inside a square of side 70 cm.
Work out the area of the shaded part of the diagram.
Give your answer correct to 3 significant figures.

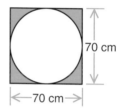

Edexcel

6 A mat is made in the shape of a rectangle with a semicircle
added at one end.
The width of the mat is 1.52 metres.
The length of the mat is 1.86 metres.
Calculate the area of the mat.
Give your answer in square metres, correct to 2 decimal places.

Edexcel

7 Each wheel on Hannah's bicycle has a radius of 15 cm.
Calculate how many complete revolutions each wheel makes when Hannah cycles 100 metres.

8 A table has a top in the shape of a circle with a radius of 45 centimetres.
(a) Calculate the area of the circular table top.

The base of the table is also in the shape of a circle.
The circumference of this circle is 110 centimetres.
(b) Calculate the diameter of the base of the table.

Edexcel

9 Three circles overlap, as shown.
The largest circle has a diameter of 12 cm.
The ratio of the diameters $x : y$ is 1 : 2.
Calculate the shaded area.
Give your answer in terms of π.

10 A circle has an area of 100 cm².
Calculate the circumference of the circle.
Give your answer correct to three significant figures.

11 Alfie says, "A semi-circle with a radius of 10 cm has a larger area than a whole circle with half the radius." Is he correct? You **must** show working to justify your answer.

Loci and Constructions

What you need to know

- The path of a point which moves according to a rule is called a **locus**.

- The word **loci** is used when we talk about more than one locus.

- You should be able to draw the locus of a point which moves according to a given rule.

  Eg 1 A ball is rolled along this zig-zag. Draw the locus of *P*, the centre of the ball, as it is rolled along.

- Using a ruler and compasses you should be able to carry out the **constructions** below.

1 **The perpendicular bisector of a line.**

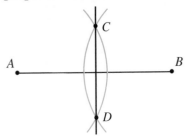

Points on the line *CD* are **equidistant** from the points *A* and *B*.

2 **The bisector of an angle.**

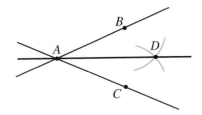

Points on the line *AD* are **equidistant** from the lines *AB* and *AC*.

3 **The perpendicular from a point to a line.**

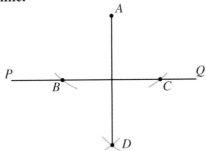

4 **The perpendicular from a point on a line.**

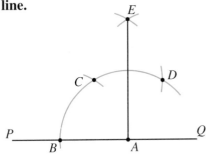

- You should be able to solve loci problems which involve using these constructions.

  Eg 2 *P* is a point inside triangle *ABC* such that:
  (i)   *P* is equidistant from points *A* and *B*,
  (ii) *P* is equidistant from lines *AB* and *BC*.
  Find the position of *P*.

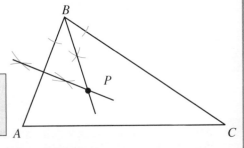

  > To find point *P*:
  > (i) construct the perpendicular bisector of line *AB*,
  > (ii) construct the bisector of angle *ABC*.

  P is at the point where these lines intersect.

1 The ball is rolled along the zig-zag.
Copy the diagram and draw the locus of the centre of the ball as it is rolled from X to Y.

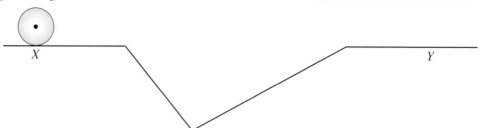

2 The diagram represents a box which is to be moved across a floor, XY.

Scale 1 cm to 10 cm

$AD = 30\,\text{cm}$ and $AB = 20\,\text{cm}$.
First the box is rotated about the point A so that BC becomes vertical.
Then the box is rotated about the new position of the point B so that CD becomes vertical.
(a)   Copy the diagram and make a scale drawing of the locus of the point C.
(b)   Find the maximum height of C above the floor.   Edexcel

3 The map shows the positions of three villages A, B and C.
The map has been drawn to a scale of 1 cm to 2 km.

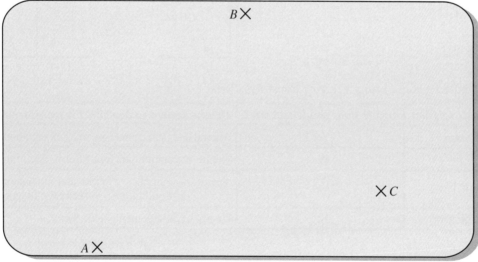

A supermarket is equidistant from villages A, B and C.
(a)   Copy the map and find the position of the supermarket on your diagram.
(b)   How many kilometres is the supermarket from village A?

4 (a)   Construct a kite $PQRS$ in which $PQ = PS = 7\,\text{cm}$, $QR = RS = 5\,\text{cm}$
and the diagonal $QS = 6\,\text{cm}$.
X is a point inside the kite such that:
(i) X is equidistant from P and Q.
(ii) X is equidistant from sides PQ and PS.
(b)   By constructing the loci for (i) and (ii) find the position of X.
(c)   Measure the distance PX.

What you need to know

- The movement of a shape from one position to another is called a **transformation**.

- **Single transformations** can be described in terms of a reflection, a rotation, a translation or an enlargement.

- **Reflection**: The image of the shape is the same distance from the mirror line as the original.

- **Rotation**: All points are turned through the same angle about the same point, called a centre of rotation.

- **Translation**: All points are moved the same distance in the same direction without turning.

- **Enlargement**: All lengths are multiplied by a scale factor.

Scale factor $= \dfrac{\text{new length}}{\text{original length}}$ | New length = scale factor $\times$ original length |

The size of the original shape is:
  increased by using a scale factor greater than 1,
  reduced by using a scale factor which is a fraction, i.e. between 0 and 1.

- You should be able to draw the transformation of a shape.

  Eg 1 Draw the image of triangle P after it

  has been translated with vector $\begin{pmatrix} -3 \\ 2 \end{pmatrix}$.

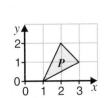
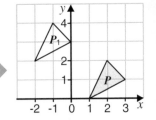

- You should be able to fully describe transformations.

Transformation	Image same shape and size?	Details needed to describe the transformation
Reflection	Yes	Mirror line, sometimes given as an equation.
Rotation	Yes	Centre of rotation, amount of turn, direction of turn.
Translation	Yes	Vector: top number = horizontal movement, bottom number = vertical movement.
Enlargement	No	Centre of enlargement, scale factor.

  Eg 2 Describe the single transformation which maps
    (a) A onto B,
    (b) A onto C,
    (c) A onto D,
    (d) D onto E.

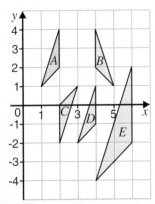

    (a) **reflection** in the line $x = 3$.

    (b) **rotation** of $180°$ about $(2, 1)$.

    (c) **translation** with vector $\begin{pmatrix} 2 \\ -3 \end{pmatrix}$.

    (d) **enlargement** scale factor 2, centre $(2, 0)$.

1 Copy each diagram and draw the transformation given.

(a) Reflect the shape in the *x* axis.

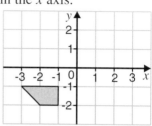

(b) Translate the shape, 2 units left and 3 units up.

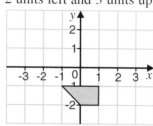

(c) Rotate the shape, 90° clockwise about the origin.

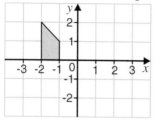

2 In each diagram *A* is mapped onto *B* by a single transformation. Describe each transformation.

(a)

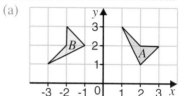

(b)

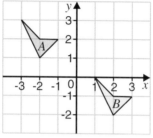

(c)

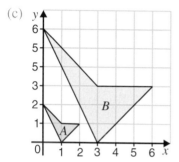

3 The diagram shows the positions of kites *P*, *Q*, *R* and *S*.

(a) (i) *P* is mapped onto *Q* by a reflection. What is the equation of the line of reflection?

(ii) *P* is mapped onto *R* by a translation. What is the vector of the translation?

(iii) *P* is mapped onto *S* by an enlargement. What is the centre and scale factor of the enlargement?

(b) *P* is mapped onto *T* by a rotation through 90° clockwise about $(1, -2)$. On squared paper, copy *P* and draw the position of *T*.

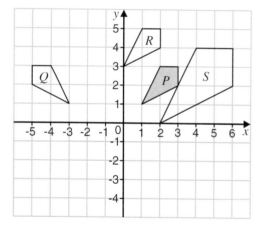

4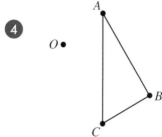

Triangle *ABC* is mapped onto triangle *PQR*, by an enlargement, centre *O*, scale factor 3. Copy the diagram and draw triangle *PQR*.

5 (a) Describe fully the single transformation which takes shape *A* onto shape *B*.

(b) Describe fully the single transformation which takes shape *A* onto shape *C*.

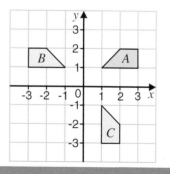

Edexcel

Transformations . . . Transformations . . . Transformations . . . . .

6 Describe fully the single transformation which maps *ABCD* onto *PQRS*.

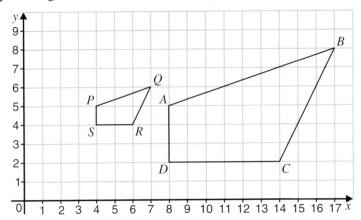

7 Copy triangle *A* onto squared paper.

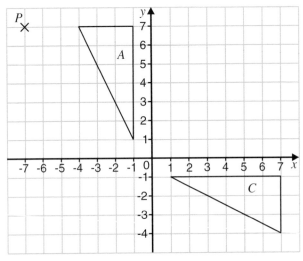

(a) Enlarge triangle *A* by the scale factor $\frac{1}{3}$ with centre the point *P* $(-7, 7)$.

(b) Describe fully the single transformation which maps triangle *A* onto triangle *C*.

Edexcel

8 (a) Describe fully the single transformation which maps shape *P* onto shape *Q*.

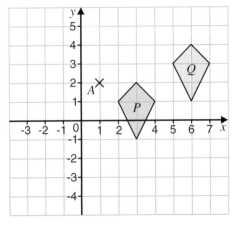

Copy shape *P* onto squared paper.
(b) Rotate shape *P* through 90° anticlockwise about the point *A* (1, 2).

Volumes and Surface Areas

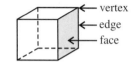

What you need to know

- **Faces**, **vertices** (corners) and **edges**.

  | A cube has 6 faces, 8 vertices and 12 edges. |

- A **net** can be used to make a solid shape.

  Eg 1 Draw a net of a cube.

- **Isometric paper** is used to make 2-dimensional drawings of 3-dimensional shapes.

  Eg 2 Draw a cube of edge 2 cm on isometric paper.

- **Plans and Elevations**
  The view of a 3-dimensional shape looking from above is called a **plan**.
  The view of a 3-dimensional shape from the front or sides is called an **elevation**.

  Eg 3 Draw diagrams to show the plan and elevation from **X**, for this 3-dimensional shape.

  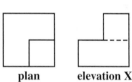

  plan   elevation X

  | Dotted lines are used to show hidden edges. |

- **Volume** is the amount of space occupied by a 3-dimensional shape.

- The formula for the volume of a **cuboid** is:
  Volume = length × breadth × height
  $V = l \times b \times h$

  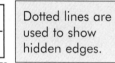

- Volume of a **cube** is: $V = l^3$

- To find the **surface area** of a cuboid, find the areas of the 6 rectangular faces and add the answers together.

  Eg 4 Find the volume and surface area of a cuboid measuring 7 cm by 5 cm by 3 cm.

  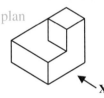

  Volume = lbh
  = 7 cm × 5 cm × 3 cm
  = 105 cm³

  Surface area = $(2 \times 7 \times 5) + (2 \times 5 \times 3) + (2 \times 3 \times 7)$
  = 70 + 30 + 42
  = 142 cm²

  Eg 5 This cuboid has a volume of 75 cm³.
  Calculate the height, h, of the cuboid.
  Volume = lbh
  $75 = 6 \times 5 \times h$
  $h = \frac{75}{30}$
  $h = 2.5$ cm

  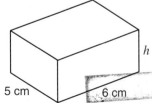

- **Prisms**
  If you make a cut at right angles to the length of a
  prism you will always get the same cross-section.

Triangular prism

cross-section

length

- Volume of a prism = area of cross-section × length

- A **cylinder** is a prism.
  Volume of a cylinder is: $V = \pi \times r^2 \times h$

  Surface area of a cylinder is:
    Surface area $= 2\pi r^2 + 2\pi r h$

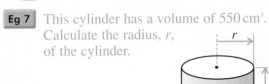

Eg 6	Calculate the volume of this cylinder.

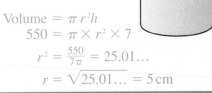

4 cm

6 cm

Volume $= \pi r^2 h$
$= \pi \times 4 \times 4 \times 6$
$= 301.592\ldots$
$= 302\,\text{cm}^3$, correct to 3 s.f.

Eg 7	This cylinder has a volume of $550\,\text{cm}^3$.

Calculate the radius, r,
of the cylinder.

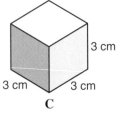

r

7 cm

Volume $= \pi r^2 h$
$550 = \pi \times r^2 \times 7$
$r^2 = \frac{550}{7\pi} = 25.01\ldots$
$r = \sqrt{25.01\ldots} = 5\,\text{cm}$

Exercise 29   Do not use a calculator for question 1.

1 (a) Which of these cuboids has the largest volume?
   Show all your working.

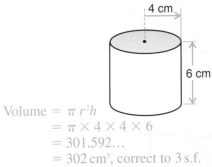

2 cm
3 cm   4 cm
A

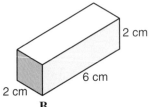

2 cm
6 cm
2 cm
B

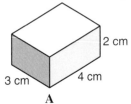

3 cm
3 cm   3 cm
C

   (b) (i) Draw an accurate net of cuboid **A**.   (ii) Find the total surface area of cuboid **A**.
   (c) Which cuboid has the largest surface area?

2 Which of these nets is the net of a pyramid?

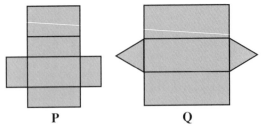

P   **Q**

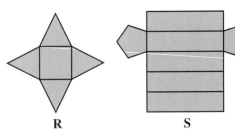

R   **S**

3 The diagram represents the babies' pool, with paving around, at a leisure centre.
   The pool is rectangular, 8 m long by 5 m wide
   and has a depth of 0.6 m throughout.

   (a) Work out the volume of the pool in m³.

   The paving around the pool is 2 m wide.
   (b) Work out the area of the paving.

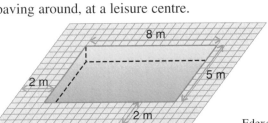

8 m
2 m
5 m
2 m

Edexcel

4 The diagram shows a cylinder.
The height of the cylinder is 26.3 cm.
The diameter of the base of the cylinder is 8.6 cm.

Calculate the volume of the cylinder.
Give your answer correct to 3 significant figures.

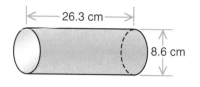

Edexcel

5 A triangular prism has dimensions, as shown.

(a) Calculate the total surface area of the prism.

(b) Calculate the volume of the prism.

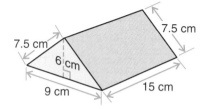

6

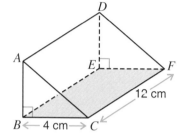

The diagram shows a triangular prism.

$BC = 4$ cm, $CF = 12$ cm and angle $ABC = 90°$.

The volume of the triangular prism is 84 cm³.
Work out the length of the side AB of the prism.

Edexcel

7 The diagram shows a solid drawn on isometric paper.

(a) Draw the plan of the solid.

(b) Draw the elevation of the solid from the direction shown by the arrow.

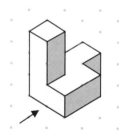

8

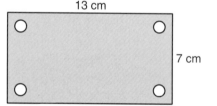

The diagram shows a rectangular metal plate with four circular holes.
The metal plate measures 13 cm by 7 cm and is 0.3 cm thick.
The radius of each circle is 0.4 cm.
Calculate the volume of the metal.

9 The diagram represents a swimming pool.
The pool has vertical sides.
The pool is 8 m wide.

(a) Calculate the area of the shaded cross-section.

The swimming pool is completely filled with water.

(b) Calculate the volume of water in the pool.

64 m³ of water leaks out of the pool.

(c) Calculate the distance by which the water level falls.

Edexcel

10 A cylindrical water tank has radius 40 cm and height 90 cm.

(a) Calculate the total surface area of the tank.

A full tank of water is used to fill a paddling pool.

(b) The paddling pool is a cylinder with diameter 2.4 metres.
Calculate the depth of water in the pool.

SECTION 30 — Enlargements and Similar Figures

What you need to know

- When a shape is **enlarged**: all **lengths** are multiplied by a **scale factor**,
  angles remain unchanged.

> All circles are similar to each other.
> All squares are similar to each other.

- When two figures are **similar**:
  their **shapes** are the same,
  their **angles** are the same,
  corresponding **lengths** are in the same ratio,
  this ratio is the **scale factor** of the enlargement.

> Scale factor $= \dfrac{\text{new length}}{\text{original length}}$

- For **similar triangles**:
  corresponding lengths are opposite
  equal angles,
  the scale factor is the ratio of the
  corresponding sides.

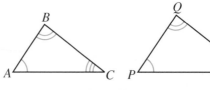

$$\frac{AB}{PQ} = \frac{BC}{QR} = \frac{CA}{RP} = \text{scale factor}$$

- You should be able to find corresponding lengths in similar triangles.

  Eg 1 These two triangles are similar.
  Find the lengths of the sides marked x and y.

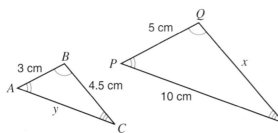

> AB and PQ are corresponding sides.
> Scale factor $= \dfrac{PQ}{AB} = \dfrac{5}{3}$

$x = 4.5 \times \frac{5}{3} = 7.5\,\text{cm}$

$y = 10 \div \frac{5}{3} = 6\,\text{cm}$

Exercise 30

The diagrams in this exercise have not been drawn accurately.

1 These triangles are similar.

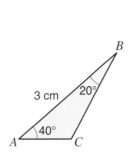

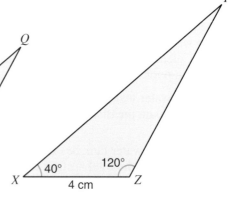

(a) Work out the length of the side XY.
(b) Work out the length of the side AC.

74

2 The diagram shows rectangles **A**, **B** and **C**.

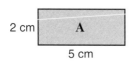 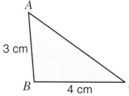 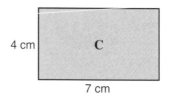

2 cm | **A** |
5 cm

3 cm | **B** |

4 cm | **C** |
7 cm

(a) Explain why rectangles **A** and **C** are **not** similar.
(b) Rectangles **A** and **B** are similar.
   Work out the length of rectangle **B**.

3 Triangle *ABC* is similar to triangle *PQR*.
Angle *ABC* = angle *PQR*.
Angle *ACB* = angle *PRQ*.

Calculate the length of
(a) *PQ*,   (b) *AC*.

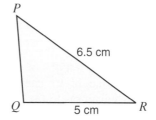

A
3 cm
B   4 cm   *C*

P
6.5 cm
Q   5 cm   *R*

Edexcel

4 The "size" of a television screen is the length of a diagonal of the screen.
The width of a 19 inch television screen is 16.2 inches.
Calculate the width of a similar 23 inch screen.   Edexcel

5 *AB* : *AC* = 1 : 3.

(a) Work out the length of *CD*.
(b) Work out the length of *BC*.

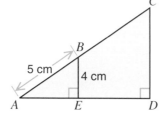

C
B
5 cm   4 cm
A   *E*   *D*

Edexcel

6 In the diagram *ABC* and *AED* are straight lines.
BE is parallel to *CD*.

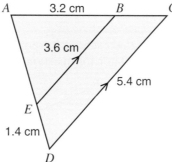

A   3.2 cm   *B*   *C*
3.6 cm
5.4 cm
E
1.4 cm
D

(a) Explain why triangles *ABE* and *ACD* are similar.

AB = 3.2 cm, *BE* = 3.6 cm, *ED* = 1.4 cm and *DC* = 5.4 cm.
(b) Calculate (i) the length of *AC*,   (ii) the length of *AE*.

7 In the diagram, *AB* is parallel to *DE*.
AB = 4.5 cm, *AC* = 2.7 cm and *CE* = 2.4 cm.

(a) Explain why triangle *ABC* is similar to triangle *EDC*.
(b) Calculate the length of *DE*.

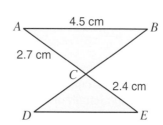

A   4.5 cm   *B*
2.7 cm
C
2.4 cm
D   *E*

Enlargements and Similar Figures

Pythagoras' Theorem

What you need to know

- The longest side in a right-angled triangle is called the **hypotenuse**.

- The **Theorem of Pythagoras** states:
  "In any right-angled triangle the square on the hypotenuse is equal to the sum of the squares on the other two sides."
  $$a^2 = b^2 + c^2$$

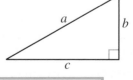

- When we know the lengths of two sides of a right-angled triangle, we can use the Theorem of Pythagoras to find the length of the third side.

$$a^2 = b^2 + c^2$$
Rearranging gives:
$$b^2 = a^2 - c^2$$
$$c^2 = a^2 - b^2$$

Eg 1 Calculate the length of side a, correct to 1 d.p.

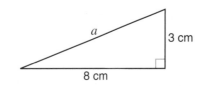

$$a^2 = b^2 + c^2$$
$$a^2 = 8^2 + 3^2$$
$$a^2 = 64 + 9 = 73$$
$$a = \sqrt{73} = 8.544\ldots$$
$$a = 8.5\text{ cm, correct to 1 d.p.}$$

Eg 2 Calculate the length of side b, correct to 1 d.p.

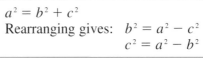

$$b^2 = a^2 - c^2$$
$$b^2 = 9^2 - 7^2$$
$$b^2 = 81 - 49 = 32$$
$$b = \sqrt{32} = 5.656\ldots$$
$$b = 5.7\text{ cm, correct to 1 d.p.}$$

Exercise 31

The diagrams in this exercise have not been drawn accurately.
Do not use a calculator for questions 1 and 2.

1 ABC is a right-angled triangle.
$AB = 5$ cm and $AC = 12$ cm.
Calculate the length of BC.

2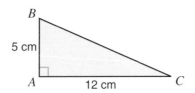

The diagram shows the cross-section of the roof of a house.
The width of the house, PR, is 10 m.
$QR = 6$ m and angle $PQR = 90°$.
Calculate the length of PQ.

3 The diagram shows a rectangular sheet of paper.
The paper is 20 cm wide and the diagonal, d, is 35 cm.
Calculate the length of the sheet of paper.

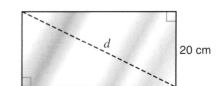

4 Calculate the length of the line joining the points $A(-2, -3)$ and $B(6, 1)$.

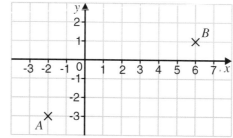

5 Three similar triangles, *OPQ*, *OQR* and *ORS*, are connected as shown.
$OP = 1\,cm$ and $OQ = 2\,cm$.

Calculate the exact length of *RS*.

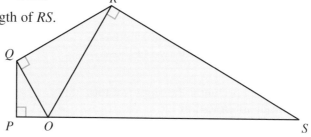

6 $AB = 19.5\,cm$, $AC = 19.5\,cm$ and $BC = 16.4\,cm$.
Angle $ADB = 90°$.
BDC is a straight line.

Calculate the length of *AD*.
Give your answer in centimetres, correct to 1 decimal place.

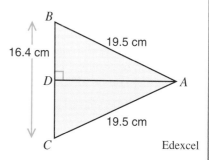

Edexcel

7

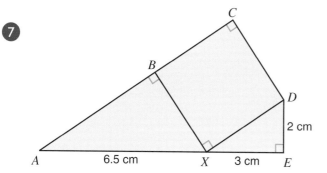

In the diagram, *BCDX* is a square.
AXE is a straight line with $AX = 6.5\,cm$
and $XE = 3\,cm$. $DE = 2\,cm$.

(a) Calculate the area of *BCDX*.
(b) Calculate the length of *AB*,
correct to one decimal place.

8 The diagram shows a sketch of a triangle.
Work out the perimeter of the triangle.

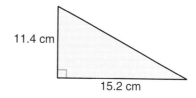

Edexcel

9

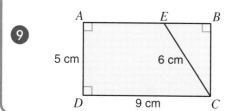

ABCD is a rectangle.
$AD = 5\,cm$, $DC = 9\,cm$ and $EC = 6\,cm$.
Calculate the length of *AE*, correct to one decimal place.

Pythagoras' Theorem

31

77

Trigonometry

What you need to know

- **Trigonometry** is used to find the lengths of sides and the sizes of angles in right-angled triangles.

- You must learn the **sine**, **cosine** and **tangent** ratios.

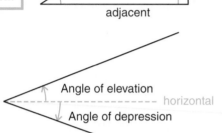

$$\sin a = \frac{\text{opposite}}{\text{hypotenuse}} \quad \cos a = \frac{\text{adjacent}}{\text{hypotenuse}} \quad \tan a = \frac{\text{opposite}}{\text{adjacent}}$$

- Each ratio links the size of an angle with the lengths of two sides. If we are given the values for two of these we can find the value of the third.

- When we look **up** from the horizontal the angle we turn through is called the **angle of elevation**.

- When we look **down** from the horizontal the angle we turn through is called the **angle of depression**.

- **Three-figure bearings**
  Bearings are used to describe the direction in which you must travel to get from one place to another. They are measured from the North line in a clockwise direction. A bearing can be any angle from 0° to 360° and is written as a three-figure number.

- You should be able to use trigonometry to find the lengths of sides and the sizes of angles when solving problems involving right-angled triangles.

Eg 1 Find the length, d, giving the answer to 3 significant figures.

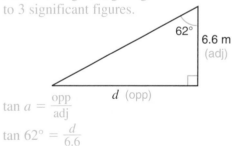

$$\tan a = \frac{\text{opp}}{\text{adj}}$$

$$\tan 62° = \frac{d}{6.6}$$

$d = 6.6 \times \tan 62°$

$d = 12.412...$

$d = 12.4$ m, correct to 3 s.f.

Eg 2 Find the size of angle a, correct to one decimal place.

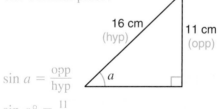

$$\sin a = \frac{\text{opp}}{\text{hyp}}$$

$$\sin a° = \frac{11}{16}$$

$$a = \sin^{-1}\frac{11}{16}$$

$a = 43.432...$

$a = 43.4°$, correct to 1 d.p.

Exercise 32

The diagrams in this exercise have not been drawn accurately.
Do not use a calculator for question 1.

1 The diagram shows a right-angled triangle.

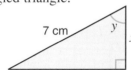

Given that $\sin\ y = \frac{4}{5}$, $\cos y = \frac{3}{5}$ and $\tan y = \frac{4}{3}$, work out the length of the side marked x.

2 Calculate the length of the side *AB* in each of these triangles.

(a)
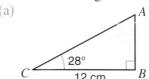

(b)
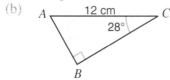

3 The diagram shows a house and a garage on level ground.
A ladder is placed with one end at the bottom of the house wall.
The top of the ladder touches the top of the garage wall.
The distance between the garage wall and the house is 1.4 m.
The angle the ladder makes with the ground is 62°.

(a) Calculate the height of the garage wall.
Give your answer correct to 3 significant figures.

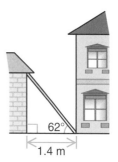

A ladder of length 3.5 m is then placed against the house wall.
The bottom of this ladder rests against the bottom of the garage wall.

(b) Calculate the angle that this ladder makes with the ground.
Give your answer correct to 1 decimal place.

Edexcel

4 Abbi is standing on level ground, at *B*, a distance
of 19 m away from the foot, *E*, of a tree, *TE*.
She measures the angle of elevation of the top of the
tree, at a height of 1.55 m above the ground, as 32°.

Calculate the height, *TE*, of the tree.
Give your answer correct to 3 significant figures.

Edexcel

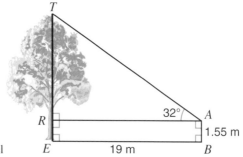

5 The diagram shows the path of a jet-ski from *P* to *Q* to *R*.

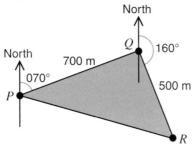

Q is 700 m from *P* on a bearing of 070°.
R is 500 m from *Q* on a bearing of 160°.

Calculate the bearing of *P* from *R*.

6 A helicopter is 200 m from a lighthouse
which stands on a vertical cliff.

From the helicopter:
  the angle of elevation to the top of the lighthouse is 15°,
  the angle of depression to the bottom of the cliff is 23°.

Calculate the distance from the top of the lighthouse
to the bottom of the cliff.

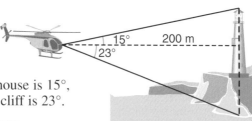

Trigonometry . . . Trigonometry . . .

Understanding and Using Measures

What you need to know

- The common units — both **metric** and **imperial** — used to measure **length**, **mass** and **capacity**.

- How to estimate measurements using sensible units and a suitable degree of accuracy.

- How to convert from one unit to another. This includes knowing the connection between one metric unit and another and the approximate equivalents between metric and imperial units.

Metric Units	**Imperial Units**	**Conversions**
Length 1 kilometre (km) = 1000 metres (m) 1 m = 100 centimetres (cm) 1 cm = 10 mm	**Length** 1 foot = 12 inches 1 yard = 3 feet	**Length** 5 miles is about 8 km 1 inch is about 2.5 cm 1 foot is about 30 cm
Mass 1 tonne (t) = 1000 kilograms (kg) 1 kg = 1000 grams (g)	**Mass** 1 pound = 16 ounces 14 pounds = 1 stone	**Mass** 1 kg is about 2.2 pounds
Capacity and volume 1 litre = 1000 millilitres (ml) $1 \, cm^3 = 1$ ml	**Capacity and volume** 1 gallon = 8 pints	**Capacity and volume** 1 litre is about 1.75 pints 1 gallon is about 4.5 litres

- How to change between units of area. For example $1 \, m^2 = 10\,000 \, cm^2$.

- How to change between units of volume. For example $1 \, m^3 = 1\,000\,000 \, cm^3$.

- You should be able to solve problems involving different units.

  Eg 1 A tank holds 6 gallons of water.
  How many litres is this? $6 \times 4.5 = 27$ litres

  Eg 2 A cuboid measures 1.5 m by 90 cm by 80 cm.
  Calculate the volume of the cuboid, in m^3. $1.5 \times 0.9 \times 0.8 = 1.08 \, m^3$

- Be able to recognise limitations on the accuracy of measurements.

  A **discrete measure** can only take a particular value and a **continuous measure** lies within a range of possible values which depends upon the degree of accuracy of the measurement.

  Eg 3 A log is 12 m in length. The length is correct to the nearest metre.
  What is the minimum length of the log?   Minimum length = $12 - 0.5 = 11.5$ m

  Eg 4 A road is 400 m long, to the nearest 10 m.
  Between what lengths is the actual length of the road?
  Actual length = $400 \, m \pm 5 \, m$ $395 \, m \leqslant$ actual length < 405 m

- By analysing the **dimensions** of a formula it is possible to decide whether a given formula represents a **length** (dimension 1), an **area** (dimension 2) or a **volume** (dimension 3).

  Eg 5 p, q, r and s represent lengths.
  By using dimensions, decide whether the expression $pq + qr + rs$
  could represent a perimeter, an area or a volume.
  Writing $pq + qr + rs$ using dimensions:
  $$L \times L + L \times L + L \times L = L^2 + L^2 + L^2 = 3L^2$$
  So, $pq + qr + rs$ has dimension 2 and could represent an area.

1 Write each of the following using a more suitable unit.
  (a)   The distance between two towns is 6000 metres.
  (b)   A mouse weighs 0.06 kilograms.
  (c)   A piece of paper has an area of 0.006 m².
  (d)   A room has a volume of 60 000 000 cm³.

2 On a map the distance between two hospitals is 14.5 cm.
The map has been drawn to a scale of 1 to 250 000.
Calculate the actual distance between the hospitals in kilometres.

3 Fred buys some apples. They weigh 3.65 kilograms.
Work out the approximate weight of the apples in pounds.
Edexcel

4 Jemma has 3 litres of milk and 20 glasses. Each glass holds one third of a pint.
How many glasses can Jemma fill?

5 Mum's Traditional Jam is sold in two sizes.
A 1 lb pot of jam costs 71 pence. A 1 kg pot of jam costs £1.50.
Which pot of jam is better value for money? You must show all your working.

6 Debbie is 5 feet 4 inches tall and weighs 9 stone 2 lb. Joyce is 155 cm tall and weighs 60 kg.
Who is taller? Who is heavier? You must show your working.

7 Last year Felicity drove 2760 miles on business.
Her car does 38 miles per gallon. Petrol costs 69 pence per litre.
She is given a car allowance of 25 pence per kilometre.
How much of her car allowance is left after paying for her petrol?
Give your answer to the nearest £.

8 The length of Andy's pencil is 170 mm, correct to the nearest 10 mm.
What is the minimum length of the pencil?

9 The distance between two railway stations is recorded as 92 km, measured correct to the
nearest kilometre. Let the actual distance be d km.
  (a)   Write down the least possible value for d.
  (b)   Copy and complete the inequality: … $\leq d <$ ….
Edexcel

10 Cleo used a pair of scales to measure, in kilograms, the weight of a brick.
The scales were accurate to the nearest 100 g.
She read the scales as accurately as she could and wrote down the weight as 1.437 kg.
Anthony said that this was not a sensible weight to write down.
Explain why Anthony was correct.
Edexcel

11 Lou has six wooden cubes.
Each cube has sides of length 10 cm, correct to the nearest centimetre.
Lou stacks the cubes, one on top of the other.
  (a)   What is the minimum height of the stack?
  (b)   What is the maximum height of the stack?

12 Some of the expressions shown in the table below can be used to calculate areas or volumes
of various shapes.
π and 2 are numbers which have no dimensions. The letters r, b and h represent lengths.

| $2\pi r$ | πr^2 | $2bh$ | πr^3 | b^2h | $r^2 + b^3$ |

  (a)   Which of these expressions can be used to calculate an area?
  (b)   Which of these expressions can be used to calculate a volume?
Edexcel

Section Review - Shape, Space and Measures

The diagrams in this exercise have not been drawn accurately.
Do not use a calculator for questions 1 to 15.

1 Find the size of the angles *a*, *b* and *c*. Give a reason for each of your answers.

(a)
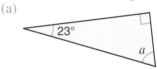

(b)
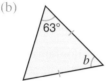

(c)
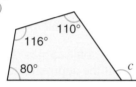

2 (a) Draw a square, a rhombus and a kite. Mark equal sides, parallel sides and equal angles.
(b) Which quadrilaterals have four equal angles?
(c) A rhombus is a special type of parallelogram as it possesses **all** the properties of a parallelogram. Which other special types of quadrilateral can a rhombus be?   Edexcel

3 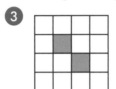 (a) Copy the diagram.
Shade two more squares so that the final diagram has line symmetry only.
(b) Make another copy of the diagram.
Shade two more squares so that the final diagram has rotational symmetry only.

4 (a) Part of a tessellation of triangles is shown.
Copy the diagram.
Continue the tessellation by drawing four more triangles.
(b) Do all regular polygons tessellate?
Give a reason for your answer.

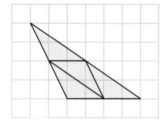

5 (a) A cuboid measures 2 cm by 2.5 cm by 4 cm.
(i) Draw an accurate net of the cuboid.
(ii) Calculate the total surface area of the cuboid.
(b) Another cuboid has a volume of 50 cm³. The base of the cuboid measures 4 cm by 5 cm.
Calculate the height of the cuboid.

6 The diagram shows a sketch of a triangle.
By making an accurate drawing of the triangle,
find the size of angle *PQR*.

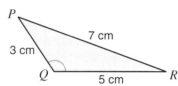

7 Use only the information given to find two triangles which are congruent to each other.
Give a reason for your answer.

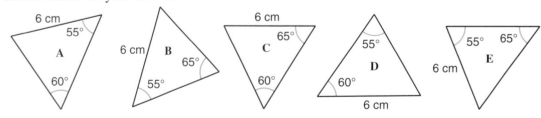

8 Colin is 5 feet 10 inches tall and weighs 11 stones.
On a medical form he is asked to give his height in centimetres and his weight in kilograms.
What values should he give?

9 The diagram shows the positions of shapes P, Q and R.

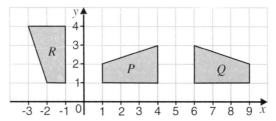

(a) Describe the single transformation which takes P onto Q.
(b) Describe the single transformation which takes P onto R.

Copy shape P onto squared paper.
(c) P is translated 3 units to the left and 2 units up.
  (i) Draw the new position of P on your diagram. Label it S.
  (ii) Describe the translation which takes S back onto P.

10 Find the size of the angles a, b, c and d.

(a)

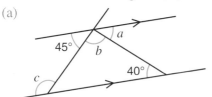

(b)

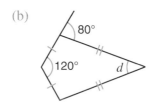

11 The scale drawing below shows the positions of an airport tower, T, and a radio mast, M.
1 cm on the diagram represents 20 km.

(a) (i) Measure, in centimetres, the distance TM.
  (ii) Work out the distance in km of the airport tower from the radio mast.

(b) (i) Measure and write down the bearing of the airport tower from the radio mast.
  (ii) Write down the bearing of the radio mast from the airport tower.

Copy the diagram.
A plane is 80 km from the radio mast on a bearing of 220°.
(c) Plot the position of the plane on your diagram, using a scale of 1 cm to 20 km.

Signals from the radio mast can be received up to a distance of 100 km.
(d) Shade the region on your diagram in which signals from the radio mast can be received.

The distance of a helicopter from the radio mast is 70 km, correct to the nearest kilometre.
(e) Write down (i) the maximum distance the helicopter could be from the radio mast,
  (ii) the minimum distance the helicopter could be from the radio mast.

Edexcel

12 Work out the area of the triangle.

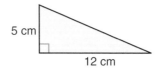

Edexcel

13 The diagram shows a square-based pyramid.
(a) How many planes of symmetry has the pyramid?
(b) How many axes of symmetry has the pyramid?

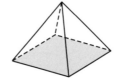

83

14 The diagram shows the plan of a swimming pool.
The arc QR is a semi-circle.
$PS = 12\,\text{m}$ and $PQ = RS = 20\,\text{m}$.
Calculate the area of the pool.

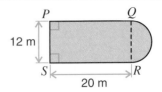

15 Plot the points $P(1, 4)$ and $Q(6, 2)$.
Construct accurately the locus of all points which are equidistant from P and Q. Edexcel

16 The diagram shows the angle formed when three regular polygons
are placed together, as shown.

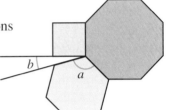

  (a) Explain why angle a is 120°.
  (b) Work out the size of the angle marked b.

17 A skip is in the shape of a prism with cross-section $ABCD$.
$AD = 2.3\,\text{m}$, $DC = 1.3\,\text{m}$ and $BC = 1.7\,\text{m}$.
The width of the skip is $1.5\,\text{m}$.

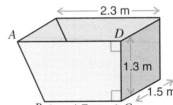

  (a) Calculate the area of the shape $ABCD$.
  (b) Calculate the volume of the skip.

The weight of an empty skip is $650\,\text{kg}$.
The skip is full to the top with sand.
$1\,\text{m}^3$ of sand weighs $4300\,\text{kg}$.
  (c) Calculate the total weight of the skip and the sand. Edexcel

18 The diagram shows Fay's house, H, and her school, S.
To get to school Fay has a choice of two routes.
She can either walk along Waverly Crescent or
along the footpaths HX and XS.
Waverly Crescent is a semi-circle with diameter $650\,\text{m}$.
The footpath HX is $250\,\text{m}$ and meets the footpath XS
at right-angles.
Which of these routes is shorter? By how much?

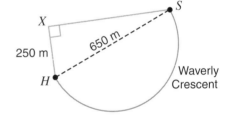

19

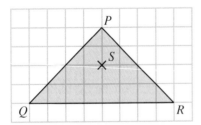

Triangle PQR is drawn on the grid.
The point S is also shown.
Copy triangle PQR onto squared paper and enlarge the
triangle PQR using a scale factor of $\frac{1}{2}$.
Use S as the centre of enlargement.

Edexcel

20 Ballymena is due West of Larne.
Woodburn is $15\,\text{km}$ due South of Larne.
Ballymena is $32\,\text{km}$ from Woodburn.

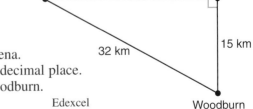

  (a) Calculate the distance of Larne from Ballymena.
      Give your answer in kilometres, correct to 1 decimal place.
  (b) Calculate the bearing of Ballymena from Woodburn.
Edexcel

21 A circle has an area of $49\,\pi\,\text{cm}^2$.
Calculate the circumference of the circle, in terms of π.

22 Copy the diagram onto squared paper.

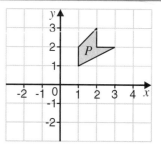

(a) P is mapped onto Q by an enlargement, scale factor 2, centre $(-1, 3)$. Draw and label Q.

(b) P is mapped onto R by a translation with vector $\begin{pmatrix} -3 \\ 2 \end{pmatrix}$. Draw and label R.

(c) Describe the single transformation which maps Q onto R.

23 The following formulae represent certain quantities connected with containers, where a, b and c are dimensions.

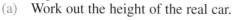

$$\pi a \qquad abc \qquad \sqrt{a^2 - c^2} \qquad \pi a^2 b \qquad 2(a + b + c)$$

(a) Explain why abc represents a volume.

(b) Which of these formulae represent lengths?

24 Simone made a scale model of a "hot rod" car on a scale of 1 to 12.5. The height of the model car is 10 cm.

(a) Work out the height of the real car.

The length of the real car is 5 m.

(b) Work out the length of the model car. Give your answer in centimetres.

The angle the windscreen made with the bonnet on the real car is $140°$.

(c) What is the angle the windscreen makes with the bonnet on the model car?

The width of the windscreen in the real car is 119 cm, correct to the nearest centimetre.

(d) Write down the smallest length this measurement could be.

Edexcel

25 BE is parallel to CD. ABC and AED are straight lines. $AB = 6$ cm, $BC = 24$ cm, $CD = 20$ cm, $AE = 3$ cm.

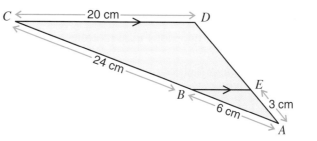

(a) Calculate the length of BE.

(b) Calculate the length of DE.

Edexcel

26 In these diagrams O is the centre of the circle. Find the size of the angles a, b, c and x. Give a reason for each of your answers.

(a)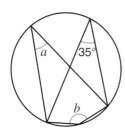

(b)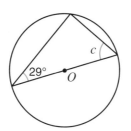

(c)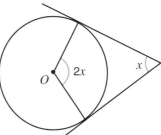

27 (a) Calculate the length of OY.

(b) Calculate the size of angle XOY.

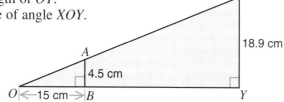

Edexcel

SECTION 34

Collection and Organisation of Data

What you need to know

- **Primary data** is data collected by an individual or organisation to use for a particular purpose. Primary data is obtained from experiments, investigations, surveys and by using questionnaires.

- **Secondary data** is data which is already available or has been collected by someone else for a different purpose. Sources of secondary data include the Annual Abstract of Statistics, Social Trends and the Internet.

- **Qualitative** data – Data which can only be described in words.

- **Quantitative** data – Data that has a numerical value. Quantitative data is either **discrete** or **continuous**. **Discrete** data can only take certain values. **Continuous** data has no exact value and is measurable.

- **Data Collection Sheets** – Used to record data during a survey.

- **Tally** – A way of recording each item of data on a data collection sheet.

    A group of five is recorded as $\cancel{||||}$.

- **Frequency Table** – A way of collating the information recorded on a data collection sheet.

- **Grouped Frequency Table** – Used for continuous data or for discrete data when a lot of data has to be recorded.

- **Database** – A collection of data.

- **Class Interval** – The width of the groups used in a grouped frequency distribution.

- **Questionnaire** – A set of questions used to collect data for a survey. Questionnaires should:
    (1) use simple language,
    (2) ask short questions which can be answered precisely,
    (3) provide tick boxes,
    (4) avoid open-ended questions,
    (5) avoid leading questions,
    (6) ask questions in a logical order.

- **Hypothesis** – A hypothesis is a statement which may or may not be true.

- When information is required about a large group of people it is not always possible to survey everyone and only a **sample** may be asked.
    The sample chosen should be large enough to make the results meaningful and representative of the whole group (population) or the results may be **biased**.

- **Two-way Tables** – A way of illustrating two features of a survey.

Exercise 34

1 Pat is investigating how long students spend on homework each night.
The time, in minutes, taken by 30 students to do their homework on a Wednesday night is shown.

| 100 | 55 | 45 | 80 | 65 | 40 | 10 | 45 | 105 | 60 | 35 | 40 | 30 | 45 | 90 |
| 25 | 120 | 55 | 60 | 75 | 70 | 45 | 90 | 45 | 90 | 45 | 25 | 15 | 20 | 75 |

(a) Using equal class intervals, copy and complete the frequency table to show this data.

Time (t minutes)	Tally	Frequency
$0 \leqslant t < 30$		

(b) Which class interval has the highest frequency?
(c) Give two reasons why this data may not be typical for these students.

86

2 A newspaper headline states: | More students eat less for breakfast. |

You are asked to investigate this headline.
Design an observation sheet to collect the data you need.
Invent the first 10 entries on your data sheet.

3 Jamie is investigating the use made of his college library.
Here is part of his questionnaire:

> **Library Questionnaire**
> 1. How old are you? ....

(a) (i) Give a reason why this question is unsuitable.
(ii) Rewrite the question so that it could be included.
(b) Jamie asks the librarian to give the questionnaires to students when they borrow books.
(i) Give reasons why this sample may be biased.
(ii) Suggest a better way of giving out the questionnaires.

4 Martin, the local Youth Centre leader, wishes to know why attendance at the Youth Centre is less than at the same time last year.
He thinks that it could be due to a number of changes that occurred during the course of the year.
These changes were: the opening hours changed,
                     a new sports centre opened nearby,
                     some of the older members started bullying the younger members.
Design a suitable question, that is easily answered, to find out why people do not attend the Youth Centre.

Edexcel

5 50 pupils are going on an educational visit. The pupils have to choose to go to one of:
         the theatre   or   **the art gallery**   or   **the science museum**.
    23 of the pupils are boys.
    11 of the girls choose to visit the theatre.
     9 of the girls choose to visit the art gallery.
    13 of the boys choose to visit the science museum.

	Theatre	Art gallery	Science museum	Totals
Girls	11	9		
Boys			13	23
Totals	19		20	50

(a) Copy and complete the table.
(b) How many of the girls choose to visit the science museum?

Edexcel

6 This sample was used to investigate the claim: **"Women do more exercise than men."**

	Age			
	16 to 21	22 to 45	46 to 65	Over 65
Male	5	5	13	7
Female	25	35	0	0

Give three reasons why the sample is biased.

7 The table shows the results of a survey of 500 people.

	Can drive	Cannot drive
Men	180	20
Women	240	60

A newspaper headline states: **Survey shows that more women can drive than men.**
Do the results of the survey support this headline?
Give a reason for your answer.

What you need to know

- **Bar chart**. Used for data which can be counted.
  Often used to compare quantities of data in a distribution.
  The length of each bar represents frequency.
  The longest bar represents the **mode**.
  The difference between the largest and smallest variable
  is called the **range**.

  > Bars can be drawn
  > horizontally or vertically.
  > Bars are the same width and
  > there are gaps between bars.

- **Bar-line graph**. Instead of drawing bars, horizontal or vertical lines are drawn to show frequency.

  Eg 1 The graph shows the number of goals scored by a football team in 10 matches.

  (a) Which number of goals scored is the mode?
  (b) What is the range of the number of goals scored?

  (a) The tallest bar represents the mode. The mode is 1 goal.
  (b) The range is the difference between the largest and smallest number of goals scored.
  The range $= 4 - 1 = 3$

- **Pie chart**. Used for data which can be counted.
  Often used to compare proportions of data, usually with the total.
  The whole circle represents all the data.
  The size of each sector represents the frequency of data in that sector.
  The largest sector represents the **mode**.

  Eg 2 The pie chart shows the makes of 120 cars.

  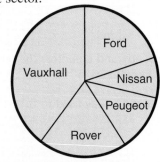

  (a) Which make of car is the mode?
  (b) How many of the cars are Ford?

  (a) The sector representing Vauxhall is the largest.
  Therefore, Vauxhall is the mode.
  (b) The angle of the sector representing Ford is 72°.
  The number of Ford cars $= \frac{72}{360} \times 120 = 24$

- **Stem and leaf diagrams**. Used to represent data in its original form. Data is split into two parts.
  The part with the higher place value is the stem.   e.g.   15 = stem 1, leaf 5.
  A key is given to show the value of the data.   e.g.   3|4 means 3.4 etc.
  The data is shown in numerical order on the diagram.   e.g.   2|3 5 9 represents 23, 25, 29.

  Back to back stem and leaf diagrams can be used to compare two sets of data.

  Eg 3 The times, in seconds, taken by 10 students
  to complete a puzzle are shown.

9	23	32	20	12
11	24	31	10	26

  Construct a stem and leaf diagram
  to represent this information.

                                                 3|1 means 31 seconds

0	9			
1	0	1	2	
2	0	3	4	6
3	1	2		

1 Causeway Hockey Club have a hockey team for men and a hockey team for women.
The bar chart shows the number of goals scored in matches played by these teams last season.

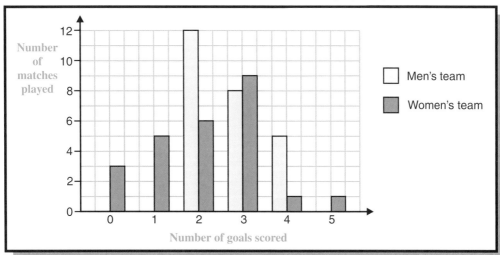

(a) How many matches did each team play?
(b) For the men's team, find the range and mode in the number of goals scored.
(c) Compare and comment on the goals scored by these teams last season.

2 The stem and leaf diagram shows the highest November temperature recorded in
12 European countries last year.

(a) How many countries are included?

(b) What is the maximum temperature recorded?

(c) Which temperature is the mode?

(d) What is the range of these temperatures?

```
                                    0 | 7   means 7°C
0 |  7   9
1 |  0   3   4   4   4   7   8
2 |  0   1   2
```

3 Derek asked 45 students to name their favourite flavour of yoghurt.
His results are shown in the table.

Flavour of yoghurt	Number of students
Strawberry	16
Orange	5
Peach	9
Blackberry	4
Other	11

Draw an accurate pie chart to show this information.

Edexcel

4

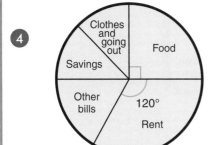

The pie chart shows how Jenny spends her monthly income.
Jenny spends £150 a month on food.

(a) Work out Jenny's monthly income.

(b) Work out how much rent Jenny pays each month.

Edexcel

5 The bar chart shows information about the injuries of drivers involved in road accidents at a busy junction.

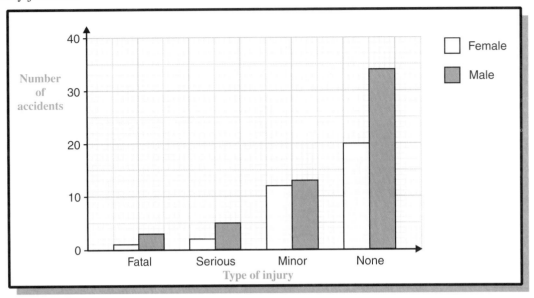

(a) What percentage of drivers had no injuries?
(b) What is the ratio of female to male drivers involved in these accidents?
    Give your answer in its simplest form.
(c) Draw a pie chart to illustrate the proportion of drivers with each type of injury.

6 Twenty children were asked to estimate the length of a leaf.
Their estimates, in centimetres, are:

Boys									
4.5	5.0	4.0	3.5	4.0	4.5	5.0	4.5	3.5	4.5

Girls									
4.5	5.0	3.5	4.0	5.5	3.5	4.5	3.5	3.0	2.5

(a) Construct a back to back stem and leaf diagram to represent this information.
(b) Compare and comment on the estimates of these boys and girls.

7 The pie chart gives information about the bills paid by a Water Company.

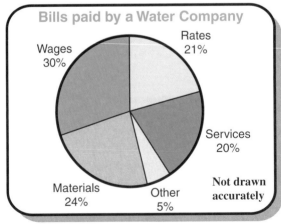

Bills paid by a Water Company

Wages 30%
Rates 21%
Services 20%
Materials 24%
Other 5%

Not drawn accurately

(a) Work out the size of the angle representing Wages.

The Water Company spent £18 000 on Materials.
(b) Work out the amount it spent on Rates.

Edexcel

Averages and Range

What you need to know

- There are three types of **average**: the **mode**, the **median** and the **mean**.

  Eg 1 The number of text messages received by 7 students on Saturday is shown.

  $$2 \quad 4 \quad 3 \quad 4 \quad 4 \quad 3 \quad 2$$

  Find (a) the mode, (b) the median, (c) the mean, (d) the range.

The **mode** is the most common amount.

  The **median** is found by arranging the data in order of size and taking the middle amount (or the mean of the two middle amounts).

  The **mean** is found by dividing the total of all the data by the number of data values.

  The **range** is a measure of **spread**.
  Range = highest amount − lowest amount

  (a) The mode is 4.

  (b) 2   2   3   ③   4   4   4
  The median is 3.

  (c) The mean $= \dfrac{2 + 4 + 3 + 4 + 4 + 3 + 2}{7}$

  $= \dfrac{22}{7} = 3.14\ldots$

  $= 3.1$, correct to 1 d.p.

  (d) The range $= 4 - 2 = 2$

- To find the mean of a **frequency distribution** use:

  $$\text{Mean} = \frac{\text{Total of all amounts}}{\text{Number of amounts}} = \frac{\Sigma fx}{\Sigma f}$$

  Eg 2 The table shows the number of stamps on some parcels.

Number of stamps	1	2	3	4
Number of parcels	5	6	9	4

  Find the mean number of stamps per parcel.

  $\text{Mean} = \dfrac{\Sigma fx}{\Sigma f}$

  $= \dfrac{1 \times 5 + 2 \times 6 + 3 \times 9 + 4 \times 4}{5 + 6 + 9 + 4}$

  $= \dfrac{60}{24} = 2.5$

- To find the mean of a **grouped frequency distribution**, first find the value of the midpoint of each class.

  Then use:

  $$\text{Estimated mean} = \frac{\Sigma \, (\text{frequency} \times \text{midpoint})}{\text{Total frequency}} = \frac{\Sigma fx}{\Sigma f}$$

  Eg 3 The table shows the weights of some parcels.

Weight (w grams)	Frequency
$100 \leqslant w < 200$	7
$200 \leqslant w < 300$	11
$300 \leqslant w < 400$	19
$400 \leqslant w < 500$	3

  Calculate an estimate of the mean weight of these parcels.

  $\text{Mean} = \dfrac{\Sigma fx}{\Sigma f}$

  $= \dfrac{150 \times 7 + 250 \times 11 + 350 \times 19 + 450 \times 3}{7 + 11 + 19 + 3}$

  $= \dfrac{11\,800}{40} = 295$ grams

- Choosing the best average to use:
  When the most **popular** value is wanted use the **mode**.
  When **half** of the values have to be above the average use the **median**.
  When a **typical** value is wanted use either the **mode** or the **median**.
  When all the **actual** values have to be taken into account use the **mean**.
  When the average should not be distorted by a few very small or very large values do **not** use the mean.

91

Do not use a calculator for questions 1 to 3.

1 The prices paid for eight different meals at a restaurant are:

£10   £9   £9.50   £12   £20   £11.50   £11   £9

(a) Which price is the mode?
(b) Find the median price.
(c) Calculate the mean price.
(d) Which of these averages best describes the average price paid for a meal?
    Give a reason for your answer.

2 20 students took part in a competition.
The frequency table shows the points they scored.
Work out the total number of points scored by the 20 students.

Points scored	1	2	3
Frequency	9	4	7

Edexcel

3 Some students took a mental arithmetic test.
Information about their marks is shown in the table.

Mark	4	5	6	7	8	9	10
Frequency	2	1	2	4	7	10	3

(a) Work out how many students took the test.
(b) Write down the modal mark.

24 students had a higher mark than Caroline.
(c) Work out Caroline's mark.
(d) Find the median mark.
(e) Work out the range of the marks.

Edexcel

4 75 boys took part in a darts competition.
Each boy threw darts until he hit the centre of the dartboard.
The numbers of darts thrown by the boys are grouped in this frequency table.

Number of darts thrown	Frequency
1 to 5	10
6 to 10	17
11 to 15	12
16 to 20	4
21 to 25	12
26 to 30	20

(a) Work out the class interval which contains the median.
(b) Work out an estimate for the mean number of darts thrown by each boy.

Edexcel

5 The table shows the number of students in three groups attending Maths City High School
last Monday. No student belonged to more than one group.

Group	A	B	C
Number of students	135	225	200

Mrs Allen carried out a survey about the students' travelling times from home to school
last Monday. Mrs Allen worked out that:

• the mean time for Group A students was 24 minutes,
• the mean time for Group B students was 32 minutes,
• the mean time for Group C students was the same as the mean time for all 560 students.

Work out the mean time for all 560 students.

Edexcel

Presentation of Data 2

What you need to know

- A **time series** is a set of readings taken at time intervals.

- A **line graph** is used to show a time series.

> Only the plotted points represent actual values. Points are joined by lines to show the **trend**.

- Variations in a time series which recur with the seasons of the year are called **seasonal variations**.

- **Moving averages** are used to smooth out variations in a time series so that the trend can be seen.

Eg 1 The graph shows the amount of gas used by a householder each quarter over a period of 3 years.
The blue crosses show the 4-quarterly moving average values.
A line of best fit, drawn for the moving averages, shows the general **trend**.
The trend shows a slight increase in the amount of gas used.

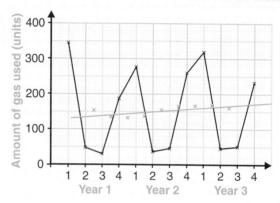

- **Histogram**. Used to illustrate **grouped frequency distributions.**
The horizontal axis is a continuous scale.

- **Frequency polygon**. Used to illustrate grouped frequency distributions.
Often used to compare two or more distributions on the same diagram.
Frequencies are plotted at the midpoints of the class intervals and joined with straight lines.
The horizontal axis is a continuous scale.

Eg 2 The frequency distribution of the heights of some boys is shown.

Draw a histogram and a frequency polygon to illustrate the data.

Height (h cm)	Frequency
$130 \leqslant h < 140$	1
$140 \leqslant h < 150$	7
$150 \leqslant h < 160$	12
$160 \leqslant h < 170$	9
$170 \leqslant h < 180$	3

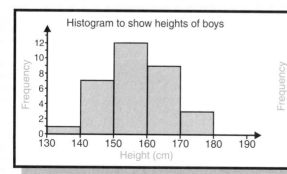

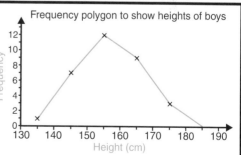

- **Misleading graphs**
Graphs may be misleading if:
the scales are not labelled,   the scales are not uniform,   the frequency does not begin at zero.

1 On Sunday, Alfie records the outside temperature every two hours.
The temperatures he recorded are shown in the table.

Time of day	0800	1000	1200	1400	1600	1800
Outside temperature (°C)	9	12	15	17	16	14

(a) Draw a line graph to represent the data.
(b) What is the range in the temperatures recorded?
(c) (i) Use your graph to estimate the temperature at 1300.
  (ii) Explain why your answer in (c)(i) is an estimate.

2 Robin had a holiday job packing cheese.
Each pack of cheese should weigh 500 grams.
Robin checked the weights, in grams, of 30 packs of cheese. These are the results.

$$\begin{array}{cccccccccc}
512 & 506 & 503 & 506 & 499 & 506 & 507 & 499 & 500 & 504 \\
502 & 503 & 510 & 508 & 496 & 497 & 497 & 509 & 506 & 496 \\
496 & 499 & 497 & 498 & 507 & 511 & 503 & 493 & 498 & 491
\end{array}$$

(a) Copy and complete the grouped frequency table for the weights. Use class intervals of 5 g.

Weight (w grams)	Tally	Frequency
$490 \leqslant w < 495$		

(b) Draw a frequency diagram to represent the data.
(c) State the modal class.   Edexcel

3 The table shows the frequency distribution of student absences for a year.

Absences (d days)	Frequency
$0 < d < 5$	4
$5 \leqslant d < 10$	6
$10 \leqslant d < 15$	8
$15 \leqslant d < 20$	5
$20 \leqslant d < 25$	4
$25 \leqslant d < 30$	3

(a) Draw a frequency polygon for this frequency distribution.
(b) Write down the class which contains the median.   Edexcel

4 The graph shows the time taken to score the first goal in 20 football matches.

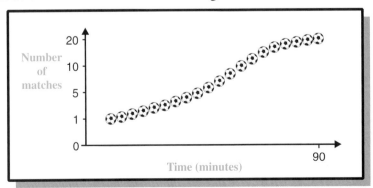

Explain why the graph is misleading.

5 The graph shows the age distribution of people in a nursing home.

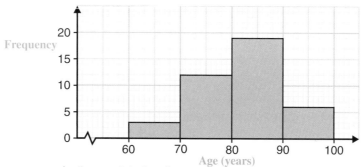

(a) Which age group is the modal class?
(b) How many people are in the nursing home?
(c) The table shows the age distribution of men in the home.

Age (a years)	$60 \leqslant a < 70$	$70 \leqslant a < 80$	$80 \leqslant a < 90$	$90 \leqslant a < 100$
Frequency	2	7	6	0

   (i) Draw a frequency polygon to represent this information.
   (ii) On the same diagram draw a frequency polygon to represent the age distribution of women in the home.
   (iii) Compare and comment on the ages of men and women in the home.

6 The frequency polygon illustrates the age distribution of people taking part in a marathon.

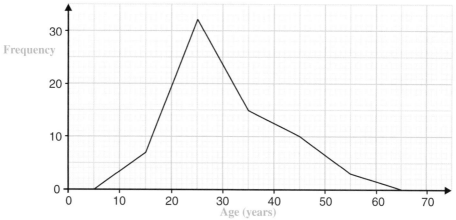

(a) How many people were under 20 years of age?
(b) How many people were over 50 years of age?
(c) How many people took part?

7 Calculate the second average in a 3-point moving average for these values.

       15   23   19   12   17   22   28   20   16

8 The table shows the number of units of electricity used each quarter by a householder over a period of 3 years.

Year	1999				2000				2001			
Quarter	1	2	3	4	1	2	3	4	1	2	3	4
Units used	680	810	470	740	640	850	420	750	970	880	490	760

(a) Plot these values on graph paper.
(b) Calculate a 4-point moving average.
(c) Plot the moving average values on your graph.
(d) Comment on the trend in the units of electricity used.

What you need to know

● A **scatter graph** can be used to show the relationship between two sets of data.

● The relationship between two sets of data is referred to as **correlation**.

● You should be able to recognise **positive** and **negative** correlation.

● When there is a relationship between two sets of data a **line of best fit** can be drawn on the scatter graph.
   The correlation is stronger as points get closer to a straight line.
   Perfect correlation is when all the points lie on a straight line.

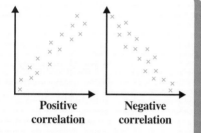

Positive correlation   Negative correlation

  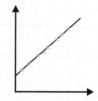 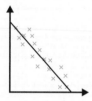 

● The line of best fit can be used to **estimate** the value from one set of the data when the corresponding value of the other set is known.

Exercise 38

1 The scatter graphs show the results of a survey given to people on holiday at a seaside resort.

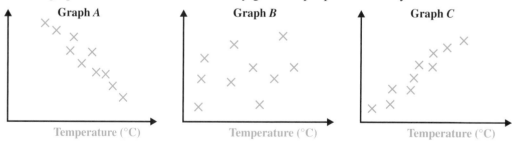

Graph *A*   Graph *B*   Graph *C*

Temperature (°C)   Temperature (°C)   Temperature (°C)

(a) Which scatter graph shows the temperature (°C) plotted against:
   (i) the number of people in the sea,
   (ii) the number of people with coats on,
   (iii) the amount of money people spend?
(b) Which scatter graph shows a positive correlation?

2 The table gives information about the engine size (in cc's) and the fuel economy (in kilometres per litre) of a number of cars.

Engine size (cc)	1800	1000	1200	1600	1400	800	2000	1500
Fuel economy (km/l)	6.5	11	10.5	8	9.5	12	6	8.5

(a) Draw a scatter graph to show this information.
(b) Describe the relationship between engine size and fuel economy.
(c) Draw a line of best fit.
(d) Explain how you can tell the relationship is quite strong.

3 The scatter graph shows the results of candidates in two examinations in the same subject.

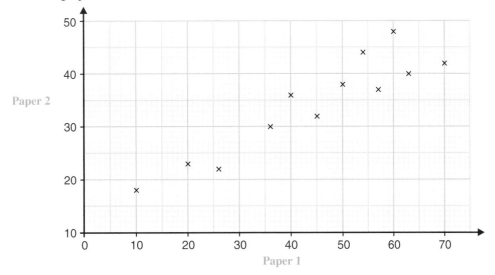

(a) One candidate scored 40 marks on Paper 1.
    What mark did this candidate score on Paper 2?
(b) One candidate scored 48 marks on Paper 2.
    What mark did this candidate score on Paper 1?
(c) Was the highest mark on both papers scored by the same candidate?
(d) Was the lowest mark on both papers scored by the same candidate?
(e) What type of correlation is there between the marks scored on the two exam papers?

4 Nine different models of car were tested to see how long it took each car to travel 500 metres from a standing start.
The times, together with the size of each engine, are shown in the table.

Engine size cc	1000	1200	1250	1400	1450	1600	1800	1950	2000
Time (seconds)	26	23	23	21	21	19	18	16	14

(a) Use this information to draw a scatter graph.
(b) Describe the relationship between the time a car takes to travel 500 metres and the size of its engine.
(c) Draw a line of best fit on your scatter graph.
(d) Use your line of best fit to predict the time taken to travel 500 metres by a car with an engine size of 1900 cc.   Edexcel

5 On seven days, Helen recorded the time, in minutes, it took a 2 cm ice cube to melt.
She also recorded the temperature, in °C, on that day.
All of her results are shown in the table below.

Temperature (°C)	9	11.5	15	17	20	21	26
Time (minutes)	63	55	48	40	30	25	12.5

(a) Draw a scatter graph for the data.
(b) Describe the relationship between the temperature and the time it takes a 2 cm ice cube to melt.
(c) Draw a line of best fit on your scatter graph.
(d) Use your line of best fit to estimate the time it took for a 2 cm ice cube to melt when the temperature was 13°C.
(e) Use your line of best fit to estimate the temperature when a 2 cm ice cube took 19 minutes to melt.
(f) Explain why the line of best fit could not be used to estimate the time it took a 2 cm ice cube to melt when the temperature was 35°C.   Edexcel

Scatter Graphs . . . Scatter Graphs . . . Scatter Graphs . . .

SECTION **39** ● ● Cumulative Frequency ● ●

What you need to know

- The information given in a frequency table can be used to make a **cumulative frequency table**.
- You should be able to **draw cumulative frequency graphs**.

To draw a cumulative frequency graph:
1. Draw and label:
   the variable on the horizontal axis,
   cumulative frequency on the vertical axis.
2. Plot the cumulative frequency against the upper class boundary of each class.
3. Join the points with a smooth curve.

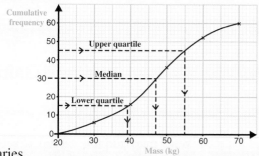

- If the question does not give the upper class boundaries, then the upper class boundary of each class is equal to the lower class boundary of the next class.
- When the classes have gaps between them then the upper class boundary is halfway between the end of one class and the beginning of the next.
- You should be able to **interpret cumulative frequency graphs**.

The **median** is the value of the middle number.
The **lower quartile** is the value located at $\frac{1}{4}$ of the total frequency.
The **upper quartile** is the value located at $\frac{3}{4}$ of the total frequency.
The **interquartile range** measures the spread of the middle 50% of the data.
Interquartile range = Upper Quartile − Lower Quartile

Eg 1 The times spent by students on the Internet one day are shown.

Time (t minutes)	$0 \leqslant t < 20$	$20 \leqslant t < 40$	$40 \leqslant t < 60$	$60 \leqslant t < 80$
Frequency	55	25	15	5

(a) Draw a cumulative frequency graph.
(b) Use your graph to find:
   (i) the median, (ii) the interquartile range.

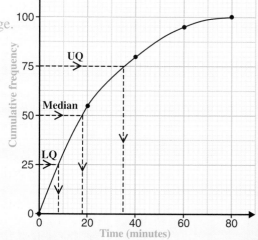

(a) Make a cumulative frequency table that can be used to draw the graph.

Time (mins) less than	0	20	40	60	80
Cumulative frequency	0	55	80	95	100

(b) Reading from the graph:
  (i) Median = 18 minutes
  (ii) Lower quartile (LQ) = 8 minutes
     Upper quartile (UQ) = 35 minutes
     Interquartile range = UQ − LQ = 35 − 8 = 27 minutes

● A **box plot** is used to represent the range, the median and the quartiles of a distribution.

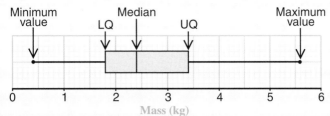

● The box plot shows how the data is spread out and how the middle 50% of data is clustered.

● Box plots can be used to compare two (or more) distributions.

● You should be able to draw and interpret box plots.

Eg 2 15 pupils were asked to estimate the size of an angle.
Their estimates, in degrees, are shown.

40　20　38　30　32　45　35　36　40　35　30　40　45　42　25

Draw a box plot to illustrate the data.

> Put the data in order and locate the median, lower quartile and upper quartile.
> Then use these values to draw the box plot.

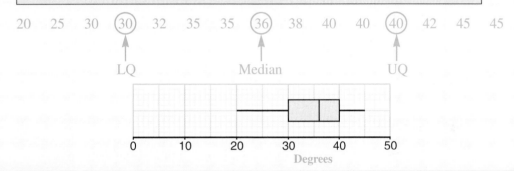

Exercise 39

1 As part of a lifesaving course a group of students were asked to swim as far as possible wearing shoes and clothes.
The cumulative frequency graph shows the distances swum.

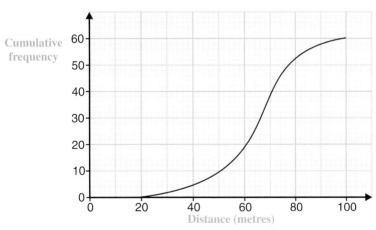

(a)　Use the graph to find:
    (i)　the median distance,　(ii)　the interquartile range.

(b)　Draw a box plot to illustrate the distances swum.

2 A group of children were asked to estimate the weight of a bucket of water.
Their estimates, in kilograms, are shown.

10	9	17.5	8	7.5	5	10	15	12.5	20	8	10	14	18	11

(a) Find (i) the median estimate,
 (ii) the interquartile range of these estimates.
(b) Draw a box plot to represent these estimates.

3 The cumulative frequency graphs show information about the prices paid for computers and televisions.

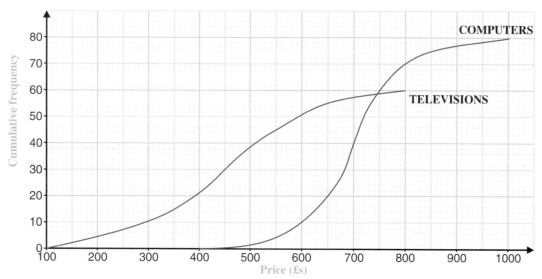

(a) Find the median price paid for a television.
(b) Find the interquartile range of the prices paid for computers.
(c) Compare and comment on the prices paid for computers and televisions.

4 The box plots illustrate the distribution of weights for a sample of eating apples and a sample of cooking apples.

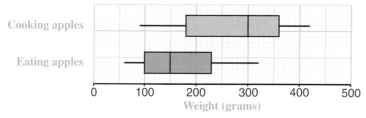

(a) What is the range in the weights of the eating apples?
(b) Which type of apple has the higher median weight?
(c) What is the interquartile range for cooking apples?
(d) Compare and comment on these distributions.

5 Fred carries out a survey of the times, in seconds, between one car and the next car on a road.
His results are shown in the table.

Time (s seconds)	$0 \leqslant s < 10$	$10 \leqslant s < 20$	$20 \leqslant s < 30$	$30 \leqslant s < 40$
Frequency	11	31	21	7

(a) How many cars were in the survey?
(b) Draw a cumulative frequency graph to show Fred's results.
(c) Use your graph to estimate the median time.
(d) Use your graph to estimate the percentage of times that were greater than 25 seconds.

Edexcel

What you need to know

- **Probability** describes how likely or unlikely it is that an event will occur.
  Probabilities can be shown on a probability scale.

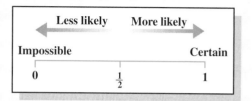

> Probability **must** be written as a **fraction**, a **decimal** or a **percentage**.

- How to work out probabilities using **equally likely outcomes**.

$$\text{The probability of an event} = \frac{\text{Number of outcomes in the event}}{\text{Total number of possible outcomes}}$$

Eg 1 A box contains 7 red pens and 4 blue pens. A pen is taken from the box at random.
What is the probability that the pen is blue?

$$P(\text{blue}) = \frac{\text{Number of blue pens}}{\text{Total number of pens}} = \frac{4}{11}$$

> P(blue) stands for the probability that the pen is blue.

- How to estimate probabilities using **relative frequency**.

$$\text{Relative frequency} = \frac{\text{Number of times the event happens in an experiment (or in a survey)}}{\text{Total number of trials in the experiment (or observations in the survey)}}$$

Eg 2 A spinner is spun 20 times. The results are shown.

4 1 3 1 4 2 2 4 3 3 4 1 4 4 3 2 2 1 3 2

What is the relative frequency of getting a 4?

$$\text{Relative frequency} = \frac{\text{Number of 4's}}{\text{Number of spins}} = \frac{6}{20} = 0.3$$

> Relative frequency gives a better estimate of probability the larger the number of trials.

- How to use probabilities to **estimate** the number of times an event occurs in an **experiment** or **observation**.

$$\text{Estimate} = \text{total number of trials (or observations)} \times \text{probability of event}$$

Eg 3 1000 raffle tickets are sold. Alan buys some tickets.
The probability that Alan wins first prize is $\frac{1}{50}$.

How many tickets did Alan buy? Number of tickets $= 1000 \times \frac{1}{50} = 20$

- **Mutually exclusive events** cannot occur at the same time.

$$\text{When A and B are mutually exclusive events:}\quad P(A \text{ or } B) = P(A) + P(B)$$

Eg 4 A box contains red, green, blue and yellow counters.
The table shows the probability of getting each colour.

Colour	Red	Green	Blue	Yellow
Probability	0.4	0.25	0.25	0.1

A counter is taken from the box at random.
What is the probability of getting a red or blue counter?

$$P(\text{Red or Blue}) = P(\text{Red}) + P(\text{Blue}) = 0.4 + 0.25 = 0.65$$

● The probability of an event, A, **not happening** is: $P(\text{not } A) = 1 - P(A)$

Eg 5 Kathy takes a sweet from a bag at random.
The probability that it is a toffee is 0.3.
What is the probability that it is **not** a toffee?

$P(\text{not toffee}) = 1 - P(\text{toffee}) = 1 - 0.3 = 0.7$

● How to find all the possible outcomes when two events are combined.
By **listing** the outcomes systematically.
By using a **possibility space diagram**.
By using a **tree diagram**.

● The outcomes of **independent events** do not influence each other.

When A and B are independent events: $P(A \text{ and } B) = P(A) \times P(B)$

Eg 6 Box A contains 3 white cubes (W) and 1 blue cube (B).
Box B contains 2 white cubes (W) and 3 blue cubes (B).
A cube is drawn from each box at random.
(a) Draw a tree diagram to show all the possible outcomes.
(b) Calculate the probability of getting two white cubes.

(a)
Box A	Box B	Outcome

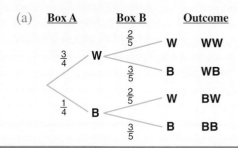

(b) To calculate P(WW), multiply the probabilities along the branches of the tree diagram.

$P(WW) = \frac{3}{4} \times \frac{2}{5}$
$= \frac{6}{20}$
$= \frac{3}{10}$

Exercise 40

1 Two fair spinners are used in a game.
The first spinner is labelled   1,   1,   2,   3.
The second spinner is labelled   2,   3,   4,   5.

Second spinner

		2	3	4	5
	1	1	2	3	4
First spinner	1	1			
	2	0			
	3	1			

Both spinners are spun.
The **score** is the positive difference between the numbers shown.

(a) Copy and complete the table to show the possible scores.

(b) What is the most likely score?

(c) Work out the probability of getting a score of 1.   Edexcel

2 The letters of the word   A B B E Y
are written on separate cards and placed in a box.
A card is taken from the box at random.

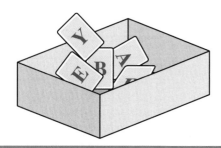

(a) What is the probability that it is the letter B?

(b) The probability that it is a vowel is 0.4
What is the probability that it is not a vowel?

102

3 Petra has 5 numbered cards.
She uses the cards to do this experiment:

> Shuffle the cards and then record the number on the top card.

She repeats the experiment 20 times and gets these results.

$$\begin{array}{cccccccccc} 3 & 3 & 2 & 3 & 4 & 3 & 5 & 2 & 3 & 4 \\ 3 & 5 & 3 & 3 & 4 & 2 & 5 & 3 & 4 & 2 \end{array}$$

(a) What is the relative frequency of getting a 3?
(b) What numbers do you think are on the five cards? Give a reason for your answer.
(c) She repeats the experiment 500 times.
Estimate the number of times she will get a 5. Give a reason for your answer.

4 Jeff tosses a coin three times.
(a) List all the possible outcomes.
(b) What is the probability that he gets one head and two tails?

5 A bag contains counters which are green, blue or white.
When one counter is picked at random,

the probability that it will be green is $\frac{1}{2}$, the probability that it will be blue is $\frac{1}{8}$.

(a) What is the probability that a counter picked out at random will be either green or blue?
(b) What is the probability that a counter picked out at random will be either white or green?

Edexcel

6 On Tuesday Jim has to catch a bus and a train to get to work.
The probability that the train is late is 0.4. The probability that the bus is late is 0.7.
(a) Copy and complete the tree diagram.

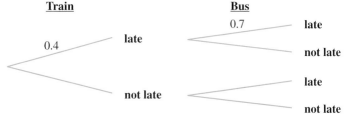

(b) What is the probability that both the bus and the train are late?
(c) What is the probability that either the train or the bus is late but not both?

7 Peter and Asif are both taking their driving test for a motor cycle for the first time.
The table below gives the probabilities that they will pass the test at the first attempt.

	Probability of passing at first attempt
Peter	0.6
Asif	0.7

(a) Write down the probability that Asif will pass the test at the first attempt.
(b) Work out the probability that Peter will fail the test at the first attempt.
(c) Explain clearly why Asif is more likely to pass the test at the first attempt than he is to fail at the first attempt.

On a particular day 1000 people will take the test for the first time.
For each person the probability that they will pass the test at the first attempt is the same as the probability that Asif will pass the test at the first attempt.
(d) Work out an estimate for how many of these 1000 people are likely to pass the test at the first attempt.
(e) Calculate the probability that both Peter and Asif will pass the test at the first attempt.
(f) Calculate the probability that Peter will pass the test at the first attempt and Asif will fail the test at the first attempt.

Edexcel

Section Review - Handling Data

● ● ● ● ● ●

1 The graph shows the distribution of the best height jumped by each girl in a high jump competition.

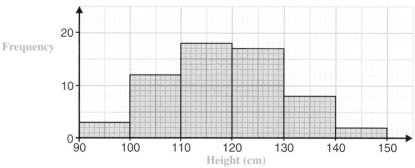

(a) (i) How many girls jumped between 100 cm and 120 cm?
    (ii) How many girls took part in the competition?
(b) Which class interval contains the median height?

2 Sylvester did a survey to find the most popular pantomime.
(a) The results for children are shown in the table.

Pantomime	Aladdin	Cinderella	Jack and the Bean Stalk	Peter Pan
Number of children	45	35	25	15

    (i) Draw a clearly labelled pie chart to illustrate this information.
    (ii) Which pantomime is the mode?

(b) The results for adults are shown in the pie chart.
    (i) 20 adults chose Aladdin.
        How many adults were included in the survey?
    (ii) Sylvester said, "30% of adults chose Cinderella."
        Is he correct?
        Explain your answer.

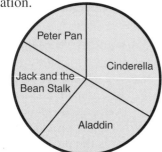

3 A game is played with two spinners.
You multiply the two numbers on which the spinners land to get the score.

This score is: $2 \times 4 = 8$

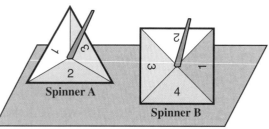

(a) Copy and complete the table to show all the possible scores.
One has been done for you.

×	1	2	3	4
1				
2				8
3				

(b) Work out the probability of getting a score of 6.
(c) Work out the probability of getting a score that is an odd number.

Edexcel

④ The names and prices of four second-hand cars are shown in the table.

Name	Nippy sports	Tuff hatchback	Ace supermini	Mega estate
Price	£12 000	£4000	£6000	£18 000

On the scatter graph, each letter represents one of the cars.

(a) Use the information shown in the table and in the scatter graph to write down the letter which represents each car.

(b) Write down the name of the oldest car.

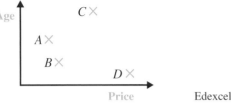

Edexcel

⑤ A packet contains 5 red balloons, 3 white balloons and 4 blue balloons.
A balloon is taken from the packet at random.
(a) What is the probability that it is red?
(b) What is the probability that it is red or white?
(c) What is the probability that it is not white?

⑥ The mean of four numbers is 7. The mean of six different numbers is 8.
Calculate the mean of all ten numbers.

⑦ Grace and Gemma were carrying out a survey on the food people eat in the school canteen.
Grace wrote the question: *"Which foods do you eat?"*
Gemma said that this question was too vague.
Write down two ways in which this question could be improved.   Edexcel

⑧ Corrin throws a dice 40 times. Her results are shown.

Score	1	2	3	4	5	6
Frequency	7	6	7	6	6	8

(a) Which score is the mode?
(b) Calculate the mean score.
(c) What is the median score?

⑨ A coin is taken from the bag of coins at random.
The probability that it is a £1 coin is 0.3.
What is the probability that it is not a £1 coin?

⑩ The lengths of 20 bolts, in centimetres, is shown.

7.4 5.8 4.5 5.0 6.5 6.6 7.0 5.4 4.8 6.4
5.4 6.2 7.2 5.5 4.8 6.5 5.0 6.0 6.5 6.8

(a) Draw a stem and leaf diagram to illustrate this information.
(b) What is the range in the lengths of these bolts?
(c) Which length is the median?

⑪ The table shows information about a group of students.

	Can speak French	Cannot speak French
Male	5	20
Female	12	38

(a) One of these students is chosen at random.
What is the probability that the student can speak French?
(b) Pru says, "If a female student is chosen at random she is more likely to be able to speak French than if a male student is chosen at random." Is she correct?
Explain your answer.

12 Ten men took part in a long jump competition.
The table shows the heights of the ten men and the best jumps they made.

Best jump (m)	5.33	6.00	5.00	5.95	4.80	5.72	4.60	5.80	4.40	5.04
Height of men (m)	1.70	1.80	1.65	1.75	1.65	1.74	1.60	1.75	1.60	1.67

(a) Plot the points as a scatter graph.
(b) Describe the relationship between the heights of the men and the best jumps they made.
(c) Draw a line of best fit.
(d) Use your line of best fit to estimate
   (i) the height of a man who could make a best jump of 5.2 m,
   (ii) the best jump of a man of height 1.73 m.   Edexcel

13 Jason grows potatoes.
He weighed 100 potatoes and recorded the weights to the nearest gram.
The table shows information about the weights (w) of the 100 potatoes.

Weight (w grams)	Frequency
$0 \leqslant w < 20$	0
$20 \leqslant w < 40$	18
$40 \leqslant w < 60$	28
$60 \leqslant w < 80$	25
$80 \leqslant w < 100$	19
$100 \leqslant w < 120$	10

(a) Draw a frequency polygon to show this information.
(b) Work out an estimate for the mean weight of these potatoes.
(c) Find the class interval that contains the median.   Edexcel

14 To collect data for a survey on the amount of milk bought each week by families,
Grant stands outside his local supermarket and asks 10 people as they leave the shop how
much milk they have just bought.
He repeats this each day for a week.
Write down two reasons why his results may be biased.

15 A factory makes boxes of cereal.
A box of cereal can be either underweight or the correct weight or overweight.
The probability that a box of cereal selected at random is underweight is 1%.
The probability that a box of cereal selected at random is overweight is 3%.
(a) Work out the probability that a box selected at random will be the correct weight.

All the underweight boxes of cereal are removed.
All boxes that are the correct weight or overweight are put in an empty warehouse.
A box of cereal is then selected at random from the warehouse.
(b) Work out the probability that a box of cereal selected at random from the warehouse will
be overweight.
Give your answer as a fraction in its simplest form.   Edexcel

16 Here is a list of the last 8 quarterly gas bills for a householder.

Month	Jan.	Apr.	Jul.	Oct.	Jan.	Apr.	Jul.	Oct.
Amount	£67	£188	£27	£18	£139	£103	£23	£27

Calculate the first two 4-point moving averages for this data.

Mr Hulme chose 10 boys and 10 girls at random from his school.
He counted the numbers of different vowels in their first names.
This table shows the results.

Number of different vowels in first name	One	Two	Three	Four	Five
Number of boys	3	4	2	1	0
Number of girls	2	3	4	0	1

There are 1000 pupils in the school.
There are 480 boys and 520 girls.
Estimate the number of pupils in the school who have exactly three different vowels in their first names.

Edexcel

 Sharon has 12 computer discs.
Five of the discs are red.
Seven of the discs are black.
She keeps all the discs in a box.
Sharon removes one disc at random. She records its colour and replaces it in the box.
Sharon removes a second disc at random, and again records its colour.

(a) Copy and complete the tree diagram.

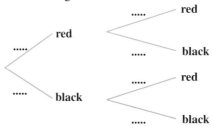

(b) Calculate the probability that the two discs removed
   (i)   will both be red,
   (ii) will be different colours.

Edexcel

19 Students in Year 11 were asked to write an essay on "Popstars".
   (a) The table shows the distribution of the times taken by male students to complete the essay.

Time (t minutes)	$10 \leqslant t < 20$	$20 \leqslant t < 30$	$30 \leqslant t < 40$	$40 \leqslant t < 50$
Frequency	8	27	19	6

   (i)   Draw a cumulative frequency graph for the data.
   (ii) Use your graph to estimate the median and the interquartile range.
   (b) The box plot illustrates the distribution of the times taken by female students to complete the essay.

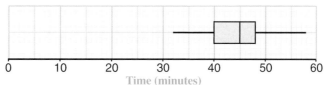

   Estimate the median and the interquartile range.
   (c) Compare and comment on the times taken by male students and the times taken by female students to complete the essay.

 Giles has two chickens.
The probability that a chicken will lay an egg on any day is 0.7.
   (a) What is the probability that both chickens will lay an egg on Sunday?
   (b) What is the probability that only one chicken will lay an egg on Monday?

Do not use a calculator for this exercise.

1 Work out 148×23.

Edexcel

2 Use these numbers to answer the following questions.

| 3 | 7 | 11 | 15 | 19 | 23 | 27 |

(a) Which number in the list is a factor of another number in the list?
(b) Which number is a cube number?
(c) (i) Which numbers are not prime numbers? Give a reason for your answer.
    (ii) The numbers are part of a sequence.
      What is the next number in the sequence which is not a prime number?

3 At midday the temperature in Moscow was $-6°C$.
At midday the temperature in Norwich was $4°C$.
(a) How many degrees higher was the temperature in Norwich than the temperature in Moscow?

At midnight the temperature in Norwich had fallen by 7 degrees from $4°C$.
(b) Work out the midnight temperature in Norwich.

Edexcel

4 Shreena has a bag of 20 sweets.
10 of the sweets are red. 3 of the sweets are black. The rest of the sweets are white.
Shreena chooses one sweet at random.
What is the probability that Shreena will choose   (a) a red sweet,   (b) a white sweet?

Edexcel

5 The time it takes to cook a turkey can be found using this rule.

Allow 40 minutes per kilogram **plus** an extra 20 minutes.

A turkey weighing $4.5\,kg$ is placed in the oven at $9.45\,am$.
At what time will it be cooked?
Give your answer in 12-hour clock time.

6 In the diagram PQ and RS are straight lines.

(a) (i) Work out the value of a.
    (ii) Give a reason for your answer.

(b) (i) Work out the value of b.
    (ii) Give a reason for your answer.

(c) (i) Work out the value of c.
    (ii) Give a reason for your answer.

Edexcel

7 (a) Work out (i) $7 - 3.72$,   (ii) $\frac{3}{5}$ of 9.
(b) What is the value of $5^2 + \sqrt{36}$?
(c) Find the value of $3x + 2y$ when $x = -4$ and $y = 3$.

8 Bruce buys two packets of baby wipes on special offer.
Calculate the actual cost of
each baby wipe.

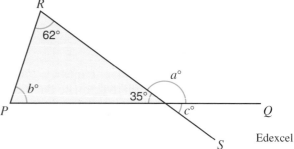

40 BABY WIPES
£2.24

Special Offer
**BUY ONE
GET ONE FREE**

9 (a) Simplify. (i) $a + 2a - 2$ (ii) $2a \times 3a$ (iii) $5a + 3(b - a)$
(b) Solve.   (i) $5x = -10$ (ii) $3x - 2 = 10$ (iii) $2x + 1 = 6$

10 The diagram represents the net of a box without a lid.

(a) Calculate the total area of the net.

(b) Calculate the volume of the box.

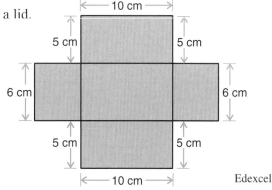

Edexcel

11

> 2 cloves of garlic
> 4 ounces of chick peas
> 4 tablespoons of olive oil
> 5 fluid ounces of Tahina paste

Here is a list of ingredients for making some Greek food. These amounts make enough for 6 people. Change the amounts so that there will be enough for 9 people.

Edexcel

12 (a) In the diagram, angle $BCD = 76°$, $AC = BC$ and ACD is a straight line. Work out the size of angle BAC.

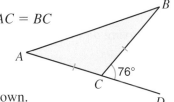

(b) Information about some triangles is shown.

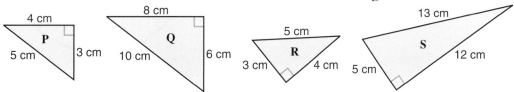

Which two of these triangles are congruent to each other? Give a reason for your answer.

(c) This shape is made using equilateral triangles. Describe the symmetries of the shape.

13 Gavin wins £48.
He gives his son one quarter of his winnings.
He gives half of the remainder to his wife.
What fraction of his winnings does he keep for himself?

14 Karina is playing a game with these cards.

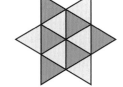

One card is taken at random from the letters.
One card is taken at random from the numbers.
(a) List all the possible outcomes.
(b) Explain why the probability of getting [X] [1] is not $\frac{1}{4}$.

15 Triangle PQR is equilateral with sides of length 60 cm.
(a) Use a scale of 1 : 10 to make a scale drawing of triangle PQR.
(b) Use your scale drawing to work out the area of triangle PQR.

16 A is the point $(-4, -1)$. B is the point $(2, 3)$. What is the midpoint of AB?

17 (a) Copy and complete the table of values for $y = 1 - 2x$.

x	-3	0	3
y		1	

(b) Draw the line $y = 1 - 2x$ for values of x from -3 to 3.

(c) Use your graph to find the value of y when $x = -1.5$.

18 (a) Work out the perimeter of this shape.   (b) Work out the area of the triangle.

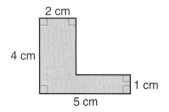

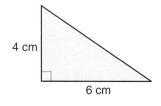

Edexcel

19 In a survey, people going to France were asked:

Where will you be staying on holiday?

The pie chart shows the results.

(a) What percentage were camping?

(b) 35 people were staying in a caravan.
How many people took part in the survey?

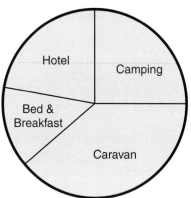

20 A bag of Estima potatoes weighs 10 kg and costs £1.80.

(a) Estimate the weight of the potatoes in pounds.

(b) King Edward potatoes cost 15% more than Estima potatoes.
What is the cost of a 10 kg bag of King Edward potatoes?

21 A bag contains counters which are white or green or red or yellow.
The probability of taking a counter of a particular colour at random is:

Colour	White	Green	Red	Yellow
Probability	0.15	0.25		0.4

Laura is going to take a counter at random and then put it back in the bag.

(a) (i) Work out the probability that Laura will take a red counter.

    (ii) Write down the probability that Laura will take a blue counter.

    (iii) Work out the probability that Laura will **not** take a green counter.

Laura is going to take a counter from the bag at random 100 times.
Each time she will put the counter back in the bag.

(b) Work out an estimate for the number of times that Laura will take a yellow counter.

Edexcel

22 A quiz has 40 questions.

(a) Grace gets 65% of the questions right. How many questions did she get right?

(b) Lenny gets 34 questions right. What percentage of the questions did he get right?

(c) 12 boys took part in the quiz. The ratio of boys to girls taking part in the quiz is 3 : 5.
How many girls took part?

23 (a) What is the reciprocal of $1\frac{1}{4}$?   (b) Work out $1\frac{1}{4} + \frac{2}{3}$.

24 Solve the equations.   (a) $11x + 5 = x + 25$ (b) $3(4y - 9) = 81$

Edexcel

25

The line *XY* crosses three parallel lines to form angles *a*, *b* and *c* as shown.
Angle *b* = 105°.
Find the size of angles *a* and *c*.

26 The numbers on these cards are coded.

| x | $2x-1$ | $3x$ |

The sum of the numbers on these 3 cards is 41.
(a) Form an equation in *x*.
(b) By solving your equation, find the numbers on the cards.

27 A cuboid has a volume of 50 cm³. The base of the cuboid measures 4 cm by 5 cm.
Calculate the height of the cuboid.

28 A farmer has two crop circles in his field.
One circle has a radius of 9 m and the other has a diameter of 12 m.
(a) What is the ratio of the diameter of the small circle to the diameter of the large circle?
Give your answer in its simplest form.
(b) Calculate, in terms of π, the circumference of the smaller circle.

29 A concrete block weighs 11 kg, correct to the nearest kilogram.
Write down the greatest and least possible weight of the block.

30 The students at Loovilla College decided to have a biscuit-eating competition.
A random sample of 25 students was taken.
The table shows the numbers of students eating different numbers of biscuits in 4 minutes.

Number of biscuits eaten in 4 minutes	1 - 5	6 - 10	11 - 15	16 - 20	21 - 25	26 - 30
Number of students	2	8	7	5	2	1

(a) Calculate an estimate of the mean number of biscuits eaten in 4 minutes.
(b) Write down the modal class interval.
(c) 250 students entered the competition.
Estimate how many of them will eat more than 20 biscuits in the four minutes.   Edexcel

31 Darren is making a pattern. He is putting white triangles around black squares, as shown in the diagram.

The number of white triangles is *w*. The number of black squares is *b*.
Write down a general rule for *w* in terms of *b*.   Edexcel

32 Draw a rectangle 4 cm by 5 cm. Construct, on the outside of the rectangle, the locus of points that are 2 cm from the edges of the rectangle.

33 A sequence begins: −1,   2,   5,   8,   11,   …
Write in terms of *n*, the *n*th term of the sequence.

34 Copy shape *A* onto squared paper.
(a) *A* is mapped onto *B* by a translation with vector $\begin{pmatrix} 0 \\ -4 \end{pmatrix}$.
Draw the position of *B* on your diagram.
(b) *A* is mapped onto *C* by a rotation through 180° about (3, 1).
Draw the position of *C* on your diagram.
(c) Describe the single transformation which maps *B* onto *C*.

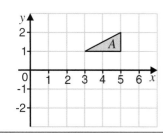

35 A youth club organises a skiing holiday for 45 children.
The ratio of boys to girls is 5 : 4.
40% of the boys have skied before.
How many boys have skied before?

36 (a) n is a whole number such that $-3 < n \leqslant 1$. List all possible values of n.
(b) In a school race the winner's time was recorded as 9.7 seconds to the nearest 0.1 second.
Let the actual winning time be t seconds.
(i) Copy the number line and illustrate the range
in which t could lie.
(ii) Copy and complete the inequality: $\ldots \leqslant t < \ldots$

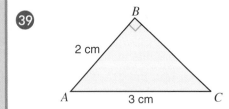
9.7

Edexcel

37 (a) Write 48 as a product of its prime factors.
(b) Write 108 as a product of its prime factors.
(c) Hence find the least common multiple of 48 and 108.

38 (a) Copy and complete the table of values for $y = x^2 - 3x + 1$.

x	-1	0	1	2	3	4
y		1	-1			5

(b) Draw the graph of $y = x^2 - 3x + 1$ for values of x from -1 to 4.
(c) Use your graph to find the value of y when $x = 1.5$.
(d) Use your graph to solve the equation $x^2 - 3x + 1 = 0$.

39

In triangle ABC, angle $ABC = 90°$
$AB = 2\,\text{cm}$ and $AC = 3\,\text{cm}$.

(a) Write down the value of cos BAC.
(b) Calculate the exact length of BC.

B — 2 cm — *A* — 3 cm — *C*

40 (a) Estimate the value of $\sqrt{\dfrac{(9.8)^3}{0.39}}$

(b) Cocoa is sold in cylindrical tins.
The height of a tin is 7.9 cm. The radius of a tin is 4.1 cm.
Use approximations to estimate the volume of a tin.
Show all your working.

COCOA

41 Solve the equation $\frac{1}{3}(2x - 1) = \frac{1}{5}(3x + 2)$.

42 The diameter of an atom is 0.000 000 03 m.
(a) Write 0.000 000 03 in standard form.

Using the most powerful microscope, the smallest objects which can be seen have diameters which are **one hundredth** of the diameter of an atom.
(b) Calculate the diameter, in metres, of the smallest object which can be seen using this microscope. Give your answer in standard form.

Edexcel

43 Solve the simultaneous equations $4x + y = 4$ and $2x + 3y = -3$.

Edexcel

44 Work out. (a) $2\frac{1}{2} - 1\frac{2}{3}$ (b) $2\frac{1}{2} \div 1\frac{2}{3}$

45 (a) Expand and simplify $(x + 3)(2x - 1)$.
(b) Factorise completely $6a^3 - 9a^2$.

Edexcel

46 Hugh buys a box of fireworks.
After lighting 40% of the fireworks he has 24 fireworks left.
How many fireworks did he buy?

47 The diagram shows the positions of shapes P, Q and R.

(a) Describe fully the single transformation which takes P onto Q.

(b) Describe fully the single transformation which takes P onto R.

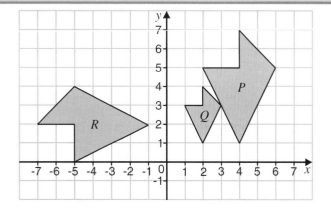

48 You are given the formula $a = bc^2$.
(a) Calculate the value of a when $b = 100$ and $c = -\frac{3}{5}$.
(b) Rearrange the formula to give c in terms of a and b.

49 Using the measurements shown in the diagram, calculate the length of CD.

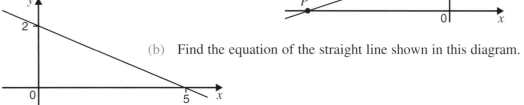

Edexcel

50 (a) What is the value of n in each of the following? (i) $y^6 \div y^n = y^3$ (ii) $y^4 \times y^2 = y^n$
(b) Calculate 3×10^5 times 4×10^{-3}. Give your answer in standard form.

51 (a) The diagram shows the line $4y = x + 5$.
(i) What are the coordinates of the point marked P?
(ii) What is the gradient of the line?

(b) Find the equation of the straight line shown in this diagram.

52 At a fete Jessie has one go on the hoopla and one go on the darts.
The probability she wins a prize on the hoopla is 0.3.
The probability she wins a prize on the darts is 0.4.

(a) Copy and complete the tree diagram for these two events.

(b) Calculate the probability that she does not win a prize.

(c) Calculate the probability that she wins only one prize.

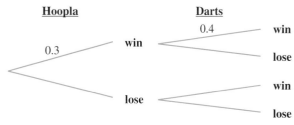

53 These formulae represent quantities connected with containers, where a, b and c are dimensions.
$$2(ab + bc + cd) \qquad abc \qquad \sqrt{a^2 + b^2} \qquad 4(a + b + c)$$
Which of these formulae represent lengths? Explain how you know.

54 (a) Factorise $x^2 - 6x + 8$.
(b) Solve the equation $x^2 - 6x + 8 = 0$.

Edexcel

Practice Exam Questions

Exam Practice - Calculator Paper

You may use a calculator for this exercise.

1 Tom Brown was going to America for his holiday.
The bank sold him £450 worth of dollars at a rate of 1.52 dollars to the pound.
(a) How many dollars did Tom receive?

Tom was unable to go to America.
The bank bought back the dollars at a rate of 1.50 dollars to the pound but charged Tom commission when it bought back the dollars. Tom received £450.
(b) How much commission, in pounds, did the bank charge?   Edexcel

2 (a) (i) Work out $\sqrt{3}$. Give your answer correct to two decimal places.
     (ii) Work out $(0.6)^3$.
(b) What is the value of m, if $47.6 \div m = 0.\dot{3}$?

3 The first four numbers in a sequence are: 15, 11, 7, 3, …
(a) What are the next two numbers in the sequence?
(b) Explain how you found your answers.

4 (a) Simplify $5m - m + 5$.
(b) Solve (i) $3x = 1$,   (ii) $4y + 3 = 19$.
(c) Find the value of $m^3 - 3m$ when $m = -2$.

5 (a) Copy this rectangle and draw in all the lines of symmetry.

(b) Show how this kite will tessellate.
     You should draw at least 6 kites.

Edexcel

6 Here is an Input – Output diagram.

(a) What is the Output when the Input is -1?
(b) What is the Input when the Output is 9?
(c) When the Input is x, what is the Output in terms of x?

7 Cheri is paid a basic rate of £5.40 per hour for a 35-hour week.
Overtime is paid at $1\frac{1}{2}$ times the basic rate.
Last week she worked 41 hours.
Calculate her pay for last week.

8 Calculate the value of   (a) $\dfrac{7.89 + 13.56}{5}$,   (b) $2.6^2 - \sqrt{6.2}$.

9 (a) Write $\frac{7}{9}$ as a decimal. Give your answer correct to two decimal places.
(b) Write 33%, 0.3, $\frac{8}{25}$ and $\frac{1}{3}$ in order of size, smallest first.

10 A bag contains 50 cubes of which 7 are red. A cube is taken from the bag at random.
(a) The probability that it is white is 0.3.
     What is the probability that it is not white?
(b) What is the probability that it is either white or red?

11 Jacob is 3.7 kg heavier than Isaac. The sum of their weights is 44.5 kg.
How heavy is Jacob?

12

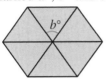

SOUP SPECIALS
Choose from: Chicken, Mushroom, Tomato or Vegetable

The table shows the number of people choosing each soup at lunchtime.

Soup	Chicken	Mushroom	Tomato	Vegetable
Number of people	16	8	10	14

Draw a clearly labelled pie chart to represent this information.

13 A rowing boat has 8 oarsmen and a cox. The mean weight of the oarsmen is 73.2 kg.
When the cox is included the mean weight is 71.6 kg. Calculate the weight of the cox.

14 The diagrams show a quadrilateral, a regular hexagon and a regular octagon.
Work out the size of the angles marked $a°$, $b°$ and $c°$.

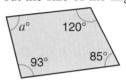

Not drawn accurately

Edexcel

15 The stem and leaf diagram shows the weights,
in grams, of letters posted by a secretary.

    (a)   How many letters were posted?
    (b)   What is the median weight of one of these letters?
    (c)   What is the range in the weights of these letters?
    (d)   Calculate the mean weight of a letter?

```
                1|5  means 15 grams
        1 |  5   8
        2 |  0   4   5   6   8   8
        3 |  1   2   3   5   7
        4 |  2   5
```

16

Gravy Granules
180 g

Gravy Granules
300 g

Normal price
54p

Normal price
90p

The diagram shows the weights and prices of
two packets of gravy granules.
This week both packets are on special offer.
The smaller packet has one third off the normal price.
The larger packet has 30% off the normal price.
Which packet is better value this week?
Show your working.

17 (a) A dinner plate has a diameter of 18 cm.
       Calculate the circumference of the dinner plate.
    (b) A tea plate has a radius of 8 cm.
       Calculate the area of the tea plate.

18 Work out $\frac{2}{5} - \frac{1}{3}$, giving your answer as a fraction.

19 This rule is used to find out how far apart to plant two bushes.

> Add the heights of the bushes.   Divide your answer by 3.

Ben is going to plant two different bushes.
He should plant them 50 cm apart.
The height of one of the bushes is 90 cm.
    (a)   Work out the height of the other bush.

The heights of two different bushes are a cm and b cm.
The two bushes should be planted d cm apart.
    (b)   Write down a formula for d in terms of a and b.

Edexcel

20 There are 2.54 centimetres in 1 inch. There are 12 inches in 1 foot. There are 3 feet in 1 yard.
    (a)   Calculate the number of yards in 10 metres.
    (b)   Calculate the number of metres in 10 yards.

Edexcel

21 The diagram shows a regular tetrahedron.
Each edge is 4 cm long.
Draw an accurate net of the tetrahedron.

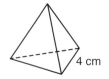
4 cm

22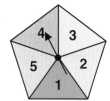

John has a spinner in the shape of a regular pentagon.
Scores of 1, 2, 3, 4, 5 are equally likely when the spinner is spun.
John spins the spinner 200 times and records the scores.
Approximately how many times will he score an even number?

Edexcel

23 Bob cycles from home to work.
The travel graph shows his journey.
(a) On his way to work Bob stopped
to buy a newspaper.
At what time did he stop?

(b) (i) During which part of his journey
did Bob cycle fastest?
Give a reason for your answer.
(ii) Calculate his average speed in
kilometres per hour for this part
of his journey.

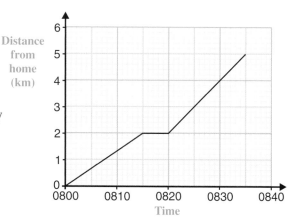

24 A hang glider flies 2.8 km on a bearing of 070° from P to Q and then 2 km on a bearing of 200° from Q to R.
(a) Make a scale drawing to show the flight of the hang glider from P to Q to R.
Use a scale of 1 cm to 200 m.
(b) From R the hang glider flies directly back to P.
Use your drawing to find the distance and bearing of P from R.

25 A regular polygon has 9 sides.
Work out the sum of its interior angles.

26 Solve the equations.   (a) $4r - 1 = 7$ (b) $7s + 2 = 5 - 3s$ (c) $5(x + 2) = 3x + 7$
Edexcel

27 The table shows the birth rate and the life expectancy for 12 countries.

Birth rate	13	17	21	25	28	30	31	34	38	41	44	47
Life expectancy (years)	75	73	71	68	65	62	61	65	61	56	51	49

(a) Plot the information as a scatter graph.
(b) Describe the relationship between the birth rate and the life expectancy.
(c) Draw a line of best fit on your scatter graph.

The birth rate in a country is 42.
(d) Use your line of best fit to estimate the life expectancy in that country.

The life expectancy in a different country is 66 years.
(e) Use your line of best fit to estimate the birth rate in that country.

Edexcel

28 The perimeter of the pentagon is 200 cm.
Work out the value of x.

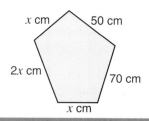
x cm   50 cm
$2x$ cm
70 cm
x cm

Edexcel

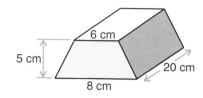

29 The diagram shows a prism. The cross-section of the prism is a trapezium.
The lengths of the parallel sides of the trapezium are 8 cm and 6 cm.
The distance between the parallel sides of the trapezium is 5 cm.
The length of the prism is 20 cm.
(a) Work out the volume of the prism.

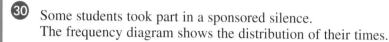

The prism is made out of gold.
Gold has a density of 19.3 grams per cm³.
(b) Work out the mass of the prism.
      Give your answer in kilograms.

Edexcel

30 Some students took part in a sponsored silence.
The frequency diagram shows the distribution of their times.

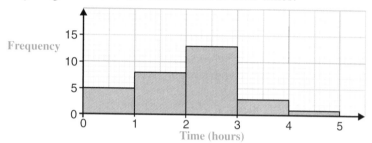

(a) How many students took part?
(b) Which time interval contains the median of their times?
(c) Calculate an estimate of the mean of their times.

31 Seth takes 2 hours 40 minutes to drive 120 miles.
Calculate his average speed for the journey.

32 The sides of a six-sided spinner are numbered from 1 to 6.
The table shows the results for 100 spins.

Number on spinner	1	2	3	4	5	6
Frequency	27	18	17	15	16	7

(a) What is the relative frequency of getting a 1?
(b) Do you think the spinner is fair? Give a reason for your answer.
(c) The spinner is spun 3000 times.
      Estimate the number of times the result is 1 or 6.

33 Bill gave his three daughters a total of £32.40.
The money was shared in the ratios 4 : 3 : 2.
Jane had the largest share.
Work out how much money Bill gave to Jane.

Edexcel

34 (a) Gerald invests £4000 at 4.5% per annum compound interest.
           Calculate the interest on his investment at the end of 3 years.
(b) Steff invests her money at 5% per annum compound interest.
           Calculate the percentage increase in the value of her investment after 3 years.

35 ABC is a right-angled triangle.
AB is of length 4 m and BC is of length 13 m.

(a) Calculate the length of AC.
(b) Calculate the size of angle ABC.

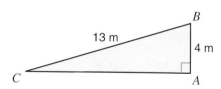

Edexcel

36 Use a trial and improvement method to find a solution to the equation $x^3 + x = 57$.
Show all your working and give your answer correct to one decimal place.

37 The diagram shows a semi-circle with diameter AB.
C is a point on the circumference.
$AC = 6$ cm and $CB = 8$ cm.
Calculate the area of the shaded triangle as a
percentage of the area of the semi-circle.

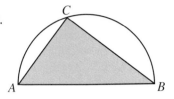

38 Use your calculator to find the value of $\dfrac{29.7 + 17.3}{1.54 \times 68.5}$.

Give your answer to a suitable degree of accuracy **and** give a reason for your choice.

39 The diagram shows the positions of three schools, P, Q and R.
School P is 8 kilometres due West of School Q.
School R is 3 kilometres due North of School Q.
(a) Calculate the size of the angle marked $x°$.
Give your answer correct to one decimal place.

Simon's house is 8 kilometres due East of School Q.
(b) Calculate the bearing of Simon's house from school R.

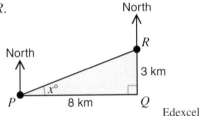

Edexcel

40 (a) The frequency distribution table gives information about the distances travelled to school
by pupils at a primary school.

Distance (k kilometres)	$0 \leqslant k < 1$	$1 \leqslant k < 2$	$2 \leqslant k < 3$	$3 \leqslant k < 4$	$4 \leqslant k < 5$
Frequency	36	76	28	12	8

(i) Draw a cumulative frequency graph to illustrate the data.
(ii) Use your graph to find the median and the interquartile range.
(b) A survey of the distances travelled to school by pupils at a secondary school gave the
following information.

Shortest distance	0.2 km	Median	2.8 km
Longest distance	9.6 km	Lower quartile	2.0 km
		Upper quartile	3.4 km

Draw a box plot to illustrate the data.
(c) Compare and comment on the distances travelled to school by pupils at these schools.

41 The volume of a cylinder is $75\,400$ cm³.
The height of the cylinder is 60 cm.
Calculate the radius of the cylinder.

42 (a) Make y the subject of the equation $x + 2y = 6$.
(b) (i) Draw the line with equation $x + 2y = 6$.
(ii) Shade the region for which $x + 2y \leqslant 6$, $0 \leqslant x \leqslant 4$ and $y \geqslant 0$.

Edexcel

43 (a) Simplify (i) $36y^6 \div 9y^3$, (ii) $4m^2 \times 3m^3$.
(b) What is the value of $2^0 + 2^{-3}$?
(c) Work out $(6.5 \times 10^3) \div (9.2 \times 10^{-7})$.
Give your answer in standard form correct to two significant figures.

44 (a) What is the gradient of the line $5y - x = 4$.
(b) Find the equation of the straight line which passes through the points $P(0, 4)$ and $Q(2, 0)$.

45 Factorise completely. $2p^3q^2 - 4p^2q^3$

Edexcel

46 Calculate the value of $\dfrac{5.98 \times 10^8 + 4.32 \times 10^9}{6.14 \times 10^{-2}}$.

Give your answer in standard form correct to 3 significant figures.

Edexcel

47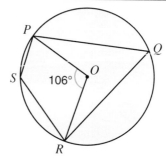

P, Q, R and S are points on the circumference of a circle with centre O.

(a) Find the size of angle PQR.
   Give a reason for your answer.
(b) Find the size of angle PSR.
   Give a reason for your answer.

48 In the diagram AB is parallel to DE and ACE and BCD are straight lines.

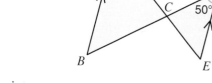

(a) Explain why triangles ABC and EDC are similar.

The ratio of BC : CD is 3 : 2.
Angle CDE = 50° and DE = 2.8 cm.
(b) (i) What is the size of angle ABC?
   (ii) Calculate the length of AB.

49 (a) Write down the values of n, where n is an integer, which satisfies the inequality $-1 < x + 2 \le 3$.
(b) Solve the inequality $2x + 3 < 4$.

50 (a) Solve the simultaneous equations $5x - 4y = -11$,
$$3x + 2y = 0.$$
(b) Factorise fully (i) $3xy^2 + 6xy$, (ii) $ma - nb - mb + na$.
(c) Multiply out and simplify $(2x - 3)(x + 2)$.
(d) Solve the equation $x^2 - 7x + 12 = 0$.

51 The diagram shows part of a roof structure.

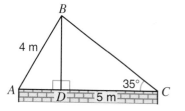

AB = 4 m, DC = 5 m and angle BCD = 35°.
BD is perpendicular to AC. Calculate angle BAD.

52 The probability of a person having brown eyes is $\frac{1}{4}$.

The probability of a person having blue eyes is $\frac{1}{3}$.
Two people are chosen at random.
(a) Work out the probability that both people will have brown eyes.
(b) Work out the probability that one person will have blue eyes and the other will have brown eyes.

Edexcel

53

SALE "30% Off All Prices".
A suitcase costs £44.66 in the sale.
How much was the suitcase before the sale?

54 (a) Simplify $\dfrac{3x - 6}{x^2 - 5x + 6}$.

(b) The diagram shows a rectangle which measures $(2x - 4)$ cm by $(x + 3)$ cm.
The rectangle has an area of 48 cm².
Form an equation in x, and show that it can be simplified to $x^2 + x - 30 = 0$.

(x + 3) cm

(2x - 4) cm

Answers

Page 1

1. (a) 1005 (b) One thousand and five
2. (a) (i) 2358 (ii) 8532
   (b) 500 (c) 50 (d) 6174
3. (a) 466 km (b) Jean's journey by 34 km
4. (a) 12 000 (b) 500 (c) 175 (d) 15
5. £181 per month
6. 50 boxes
7. (a) 18 (b) 12 (c) 3
8. 70 kg
9. 115 cm
10. 33 069
11. £6894
12. 218 days
13. (a)

End of year	1	2	3	4	5
Number of hamsters	20	60	180	540	1620

   (b) 65

Page 2

1. (a) 23.0
   (b) 0.065
   (c) 0.065, 0.9, 4.5, 13.5, 23.0
   (d) 0.065 and 0.9
2. (a) 320 (b) 0.032
3. (a) 11.37 (b) 2.9 (c) 2.64
4. (a) There are two figures after the decimal points in the question but only one in the answer.
   (b) (i) 0.12 (ii) 0.06
5. (a) (i) 4.02 (ii) 12
   (b) (i) 136 (ii) 0.0245
6. (a) 35 (b) 20p
7. (a) 560. E.g. divide by 10, multiply by 8.
   (b) 150. E.g. multiply by 10, divide by 4.
8. (a) 3.2×8.5
   (b) No. $3.2 \times 8.5 = 27.2$
9. (a) 7.36 (b) 3.2 (c) 230
10. 40 minutes
11. $0 < m < 1$ E.g. $\frac{1}{2}$, $\frac{2}{5}$.
12. 1.57 m
13. 11.5 p/kg. Bag: 38 p/kg, sack: 26.5 p/kg.
14. £3.61
15. 403 km
16. 17.76792453
17. 0.4075

Page 4

1. (a) 626 (b) 630 (c) 600
2. 19 500
3. 300 km + 100 km = 400 km
4. $\frac{3000 \times 40}{100} = £1200$
5. (a) 40×90 (b) 3600 (c) 49
6. $2000 \div 40 = 50$
7. (a) 100 is bigger than 97, **and** 50 is bigger than 49.
   (b) Smaller. 1000 is smaller than 1067, **and** 50 is bigger than 48.
8. (a) $20 \times 70 = 1400$ seats
   (b) $1400 \times £10 = £14\,000$
9. $\frac{400 + 200}{40} = \frac{600}{40} = 15$. Answer is wrong.
10. $\frac{0.3 \times 80}{5} = 4.8$ (or 5)
11. $\frac{9000}{10} \times 70p = £630$
12. 17 boxes
13. (a) 14.95 (b) 15.0
14. (a) 680 (b) 700
15. (a) 5.978 (b) $\frac{90 \times 4}{70 - 10} = \frac{360}{60} = 6$

Page 6

1. (a) $-3°C$ (b) $-13°C$
2. (a) (i) Oslo (ii) Warsaw
   (b) $-24°C$
3. $-9, -3, 0, 5, 7, 17$
4. (a) 5 (b) -15 (c) 5
5. (a) 6 (b) -1
6. 140 m
7. (a) Montreal (b) 45°C
8. £57 overdrawn ($-£57$)
9. (a) 6 degrees (b) Between 1200 and 1800
10. 7 degrees
11. (a) -4 (b) -8
12. (a) (i) -20 (ii) 21 (b) (i) -4 (ii) 3
13. 20°F
14. (a) -20 (b) -15
15. 5

Exercise 5   Page 9

1. (a) 1, 2, 3, 6, 9, 18   (b) 35
   (c) 15 has more than 2 factors: 1, 3, 5, 15

2. (a) 2, 5   **8.** 30
   (b) 20   **9.** (a) $2^2 \times 3^2$
   (c) 2, 5, 11, 17   (b) $3^2 \times 5$

3. (a) 36 (b) 10   (c) 9
   (c) 27 (d) 2   (d) 180

4. 60   **10.** 30 seconds

5. (a) 5 (b) 64   **11.** (a) 5 (b) 0.25

6. (a) 2 (b) 64   **12.** (a) 72 (b) 225

7. (a) 7 (b) 176   (c) 32

13. (a) $\sqrt{225}$, $\sqrt{225} = 15$, $2^4 = 16$ (b) 2

14. (a) $x = 9$ (b) $x = 3$
    (c) $x = 18$ (d) $x = 1$

15. (a) 3^5 (b) 4^3 (c) 5^3 (d) 9^6 (e) 2^{-2}

16. Reciprocal of 0.1. $2^3 = 8$, $\frac{1}{0.1} = 10$

17. (a) 8 and 9   (b) 8.37

18. 0.14

19. (a) 18.277415... (b) 18.28

20. (a) 46.416376... (b) 46

21. 41.2

22. (a) 10.657
    (b) $\sqrt{\frac{4}{0.2^2}} = \sqrt{\frac{4}{0.04}} = \sqrt{100} = 10$

Exercise 6   Page 11

1. 1×10^6

2. (a) (i) 2.6×10^4 (ii) 26 000
   (b) (i) 8.9×10^{-5} (ii) 0.000 089

3. (a) 5.7×10^7 (b) 5.7×10^{-5}

4. (a) 5.6×10^4 (b) 3×10^8
   (c) 1.2×10^{-1}

5. 3.96×10^8

6. (a) 2.7×10^{-23} (b) 1.35×10^{-14} grams

7. (a) Mexico   (b) 4 700 000
   (c) 1.271×10^8

8. (a) 6×10^{-6} (b) 6×10^8

9. 2.5125×10^{-21} grams

10. 4.329×10^5 kg

11. (a) 1.6×10^9 (b) 0.000 79

12. 11.1 light years

13. (a) 3.796×10^2 (b) $H = 9.94 \times 10^4$

14. 0.000 008 5   **15.** 0.007

Exercise 7   Page 13

1. (a) $n = 9$ **4.** £12
   (b) $n = 2$ **5.** 15 miles
   (c) $n = 20$ **6.** 8

2. (a) $\frac{7}{10}$ as $\frac{4}{5} = \frac{8}{10}$ **7.** $\frac{2}{3}$
   (b) $\frac{5}{12}$ **8.** $\frac{1}{5}$

3. $\frac{1}{4}, \frac{7}{20}, \frac{3}{8}, \frac{2}{5}$ **9.** £46

10. £3.92 per kilogram

11. (a) $\frac{3}{10}$ (b) $\frac{5}{12}$ (c) $4\frac{1}{10}$

12. (a) 0.167
    (b) 1.7, 1.67, 1.66, $1\frac{1}{6}$, 1.067

13. $\frac{12}{25}$ **14.** $\frac{9}{20}$ **15.** $\frac{13}{60}$

16. (a) $2\frac{1}{3}$ (b) $\frac{9}{10}$ (c) 12

17. $\frac{7}{10}$
    $\frac{7}{10} = 0.7$, $\frac{2}{3} = 0.66...$, $\frac{7}{8} = 0.875$, $\frac{9}{11} = 0.818...$

18. £120

Exercise 8   Page 15

1. 0.4, 42%, $\frac{9}{20}$ **7.** 60p

2. (a) 15 kg (b) £45   **8.** 90p per glass

3. Daisy.   **9.** £8.45 per hour
   Daisy scored $\frac{4}{5} = 80\%$.   **10.** £31.35

4. (a) 20% (b) 25%   **11.** 36%

5. 125 people   **12.** 81

6. 700 people   **13.** 15%

14. (a) 955 kg   (b) 84.4%, within 85% limit.

15. Car A. Car A: $\frac{600}{3000} \times 100 = 20\%$
    Car B: $\frac{2850}{15\,000} \times 100 = 19\%$

16. 6670 million   **20.** 32%

17. £48.50   **21.** 400

18. £14 000   **22.** 75p each

19. (a) 40% (b) £960   **23.** £60

Exercise 9   Page 19

1. (a) 53 minutes   (b) 0739

2. £29.90   **4.** £1376.25

3. £5.60   **5.** £213.75

6. (a) (i) 890 km (ii) 551.8 miles   (b) £11

7. £480   **9.** £1746.30

8. £209.25   **10.** 12 days

11. Washing Power: £247.50,   Whytes: £256.00, Clean Up: £246.75

12. (a) 64 euros   (b) £6.25

13. Small bar.   Large: 2.66 g/p,   Small: 2.78 g/p

14. £21.25   **15.** £614.68

16. (a) £360   (b) £288.26

17. (a) £3472.88   (b) 19.1%

SECTION 10

Exercise 10   Page 21

1. 8 large bricks   **2.** 7.5 kg   **3.** $\frac{3}{5}$ **4.** 4 cm

5. 150 g butter, 120 g sugar, 135 g flour, 3 eggs, 45 ml milk.

6. (a) 70%   **10.** £123.75
   (b) 9 women   **11.** £44.75

7. 20   **12.** 1 : 20 000

8. £87   **13.** (a) £76.80

9. (a) 1 : 3   (b) 20 m³   (b) £51.20

SECTION 11

Exercise 11   Page 24

1. 64 km/h   **4.** 40 minutes

2. $1\frac{1}{2}$ hours   **5.** 48 miles per hour

3. 165 km   **6.** 2.5 km

7. (a) 40 miles per hour   (b) 1116

8. (a) 1306   (b) 1000 and 1100   (c) 50 km/h

9. (a) (i) 5 km   (ii) 11.20 am
     (iii) 10 minutes
   (b) 12 km/h

10. 28.8 mph

11. (a)

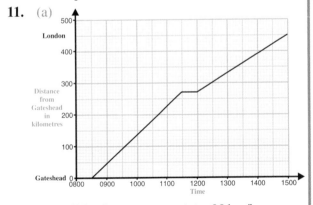

   (b) 60 km/h   (c) 90 km/h

12. 9.8 m/s   **14.** 19 g

13. 9 g/cm³   **15.** 259.3 people/km²

16. (a) 2.94×10^7 (b) 9 270 000 km²

122

1. One million

2. (a) 9472   (b) 25

3. (a) 49 pence   (b) £4.20

4. (a) 2   (b) 80   (c) 2
   (d) 36   (e) 27

5. £4752

6. (a) −4°C, −2°C, −1°C, 0°C, 1°C, 3°C, 7°C.
   (b) 11°C

7. (a) 20 × 30   (b) 600

8. £80

9. (a) −0.4, −0.35, 0.345, 0.35, 0.355
   (b) 0.45
   (c) (i) 4.74   (ii) 0.08   (iii) 80
   (d) £15.60

10. (a) (i) 100 000   (ii) 68
     (iii) 72   (iv) 0.9
   (b) 5^4, $5^4 = 625$, $4^5 = 1024$
   (c) 50

11. (a) 80%   (b) £125   (c) 65%

12. (a) $\frac{1}{2}$, $\frac{3}{5}$, $\frac{5}{8}$, $\frac{2}{3}$, $\frac{3}{4}$
   (b) $\frac{9}{40}$
   (c) (i) $\frac{13}{20}$ (ii) $\frac{1}{6}$ (iii) $\frac{8}{15}$
   (d) $4\frac{4}{5}$ or   4.8

13. (a) 8100   (b) 36 000

14. (a) 34.7   (b) 50 × 300 = 15 000

15. (a) £33.75   (b) £27

16. £55.65   **21.** (a) 16 km/h
                    (b) 1106

17. (a) 18 pence   **22.** 28
   (b) £6.48
   (c) 75%   **23.** (a) Ruth: £100,

18. 45 pence   Ben: £80
                        (b) 60%

19. £4.75

20. £1.38   **24.** 264

25. (a) $2^3 \times 3^2$ (b) $2^5 \times 3$
   (c) 288

26. (a) 400 000   (b) 2.4×10^9

27. (a) £4800   (b) £5232
   (c) £900

28. (a) 30 minutes   (b) 18 km
   (c) 36 km/h

29. (a) (i) 0.9   (ii) 0.882352941
   (b) E.g. $\frac{89}{100}$

30. 0824   **31.** 0.208569...

32. France.   England: $\frac{454}{89} = 5.1$ g/p
             France: $\frac{681}{184} \times 158 = 5.8$ g/p

33. 1.094 yards   **34.** (a) 4   (b) 51.2

35. 12.5%   **36.** £1082.13

37. (a) 5×10^{101} (b) 5×10^{-8} metres

38. 889.61 dollars

39. (a) $\sqrt{6.9}$, 2.58, $2\frac{4}{7}$, 1.6^2

   (b) (i) 290   (ii) $\dfrac{600 \times 30}{80 - 20} = \dfrac{18\,000}{60} = 300$

40. (a) £923.55   (b) £1100

41. (a) 2×10^4 (b) 8×10^6
   (c) 2.5×10^{-3}

42. 3150

43. (a) 1.728×10^7 (b) 1.85

44. (a) £2415.90   (b) £1200

45. £25 335

46. (a) 1.48×10^8 km   (b) 29.3%

SECTION 12

Exercise 12   Page 30

1. £9k

2. (a) $t + 5$ years   (b) $x - 5$ years

3. $3x + 2y$ pence

4. (a) $6m$ (b) $m + 2$ (c) m^3

5. (a) $7x$ (b) $7y - 5$

6. $5d + 15$ pence   **7.** $4x + 200$ degrees

8. (a) $10a^2$ (b) $6gh$ (c) $2k$ (d) 3

9.

$a + a$ and	$2a$
$2(a + 1)$ and	$2a + 2$
$2a + 1$ and	$a + a + 1$
a^2 and	$a \times a$

10. (a) (i) $3x + 3$ (ii) $x + 2y$
   (b) (i) $2x + 6$ (ii) $x^2 - x$
   (c) (i) $2x - 5$ (ii) $13 + 3x$
   (d) (i) $2(a - 3)$ (ii) $x(x + 2)$

11. (a) £xy (b) £$y(x - 5)$

12. (a) $3ab - 2a - b$ (b) $8x + 19$

13. $3x - 5$ years

14. (a) y^5 (b) x^3 (c) z^2 (d) y^6

15. (a) $t^5 - t^6$ (b) 30   (c) $3a$

16. (a) $x(x - 3)$ (b) $2pq(2p + q)$

17. (a) $8 - 6n$ (b) $6m^2$ (c) $2m(4n - 1)$

18. (a) $6a^4$ (b) $2x^6$ (c) $2mn^4$ (d) $20x^5y^2$

19. (a) (i) $2x^2 - 6xy$ (ii) $9a^2 + 3a^3$
   (b) (i) $2y(2x - y)$ (ii) $3m(m - 4)$
   (c) $x^2 - x$

20. $2b^2$

21. (a) $4xy - 2x^2y$ (b) $3pq(2 - q)$
   (c) $3m^3$

SECTION 13

Exercise 13   Page 32

1. (a) 15   (b) 9   (c) 5   (d) 4

2. (a) $x = 5$ (b) $x = 2$
   (c) $x = 2$ (d) $x = 4$

3. (a) 5   (b) 4

4. (a) $x = 10$ (b) $x = 6$
   (c) $x = 6$ (d) $x = 11$

5. $n + (n + 3) + (2n - 1) = 30$
   $\qquad 4n + 2 = 30$
   $\qquad\qquad n = 7$

6. $n + (2n + 5) = 47$
   $\qquad 3n + 5 = 47$
   $\qquad\qquad n = 14$
   Larger box has 33 chocolates.

7. (a) $x = 8$ (b) $x = 1$
   (c) $x = -4$ (d) $x = 2.5$

8. (a) $y = 7$ (b) $p = 2.5$
   (c) $t = 3$

9. (a) $a = 1.5$ (b) $b = 4$
   (c) $c = 5.6$

10. (a) $x = -21$ (b) $x = 2\frac{1}{2}$
   (c) $x = \frac{3}{5}$ (d) $x = -12$

11. (a) $p = 6.5$ (b) $q = 7$

12. (a) $x = 1$ (b) $x = -2\frac{1}{2}$
   (c) $x = 2\frac{1}{2}$ (d) $x = 6$

13. (a) (i) $AB = 5d + 3$ cm
   (ii) $CD = 2d + 10$ cm
   (b) (i) $5d + 3 = 2d + 10$
   (ii) $d = 2\frac{1}{3}$ cm

14. (a) $x = 1$ (b) $a = -4$
   (c) $x = 6\frac{1}{2}$

15. (a) $x = 1\frac{2}{5}$ (b) $x = -11$

SECTION 14

Exercise 14   Page 34

1. 4   **6.** $L = 8$

2. -1 **7.** $A = -11$

3. -13 **8.** 90

4. (a) 2   (b) -8 **9.** 24
   (c) 8   (d) -15

5. (a) -60 (b) 6   **10.** $T = 100$

11. (a) $m = 0.04w$ (b) 1.2 kg

12. (a) $C = 25x + 10y$ (b) $y = 10$

13. (a) $y = 2x + 1$ (b) $x = 4$

14. $c = 7.2$ **15.** $t = \dfrac{c + 5}{3}$

16. $s = -3.75$

17. $m = \dfrac{n - 3}{p}$

18. (a) $V = 1240$ 　　(b) $h = \dfrac{3V}{\pi(R^2 + Rr + r^2)}$

19. $n = 2$

20. $r = \dfrac{ps}{g}$

21. (a) $v = 12.2$ 　　(b) $a = \dfrac{v - u}{t}$

22. $s = \pm\sqrt{t - 5}$

23. $h = \pm\sqrt{\dfrac{5g}{3}}$

24. $x = \pm\sqrt{5y - 4}$

SECTION 15

Exercise 15 　　　　Page 36

1. (a) 17　　(b) 81　　(c) $\frac{1}{16}$

2. 37, 60

3. (a) 14
　　(b) No. Number must be (multiple of 3) $- 1$.

4. 5, 6, $5\frac{1}{2}$

5. (a) Multiply the last term by 3.　　(b) 405

6. (a) 28, 76　　(b) 7, 11

7. No. The sequence does not end.
　　Sequence: 1, 6, 10, 8, 4, 8, 8, 0, 16, ...

8. (a) Pattern 20 has 58 squares.
　　　　$3 \times$ (pattern number) -2
　　(b) $3n - 2$

9. (a) 19, 23　　(b) $4n - 1$

10. (a) $2n + 3$　　(b) $4n - 3$

11. (a) 120, 108, 96, 84, 72
　　(b) $132 - 12n$

12. (a) -3, 0, 5
　　(b) Yes. When $n = 8$, $8^2 - 4 = 60$.

13. (a) 38, 51
　　(b) No common difference.
　　(c) The nth term is given by $n^2 + 2$.
　　　　So, $20^2 + 2 = 402$

SECTION 16

Exercise 16. 　　　　Page 39

1. (a)

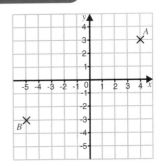

　　(b) $p = -2$

2. (a)

x	-3	-2	-1	0	1	2
y	-3	-1	1	3	5	7

　　(b)

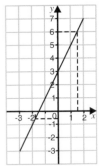

　　(c) (i) $y = 6$
　　　　(ii) $x = -1.75$

3.

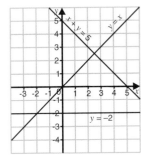

4. (a)

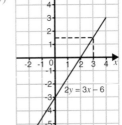

　　(b) $x + y = 5$

5. (a) $P(0, 3)$, $Q(6, 0)$　　(b) $m = 5.5$

6. (a) $x = 4$　　(b) (i) $\frac{1}{2}$　　(ii) $y = \frac{1}{2}x + 2$

7. 1: **R**, 2: **S**, 3: **Q**, 4: **P**

8. (a)

x	-2	0	4
y	-6	-3	3

　　(b)

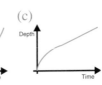

　　(c) 1.5　　(d) $x = 3$

9. (a) $y = \frac{2}{5}x + 2$
　　(b) $y = \frac{2}{5}x - 1$

10. (a) £10
　　(b) 50 pence

11. (a) (i) £31　　(ii) £48.60
　　(b) $c = \frac{2}{5}x + 7$

12. (a) 　　　　(b) 　　　　(c)

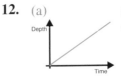

SECTION 17

Exercise 17 　　　　Page 42

1. (b) If $y = 2x$ and $y = 6 - x$,
　　then $2x = 6 - x$.
　　Find the values of x and y where the
　　graphs intersect, $x = 2$, $y = 4$.

2. $x = 3$, $y = -2$　　**4.** $x = 2\frac{1}{2}$, $y = \frac{1}{2}$

3. (b) $x = \frac{1}{2}$, $y = 3\frac{1}{2}$　　**5.** (b) $x = 1$, $y = 3$

6. (a)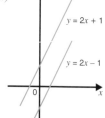

(b) The lines are parallel.

$y = 2x + 1$

$y = 2x - 1$

7. $x = \frac{1}{2}, \quad y = 4$

8. $x = -2, \quad y = 5$

9. $x = 5, \quad y = -2$

10. (a) $x + y = 40$ and $4x + 7y = 184$
    (b) $x = 32, \quad y = 8$

11. (a) $2x + 4y = 65$ and $x + 3y = 40$
    (b) $x = £17.50, \quad y = £7.50$

12. $x = \frac{3}{4}, \quad y = -\frac{1}{2}$ **13.** $x = 5, \quad y = -1$

SECTION 18

Exercise 18   Page 44

1. (a) $x > 3$ (b) $x \geqslant -2$
    (c) $x \leqslant 2$ (d) $x < -2$

2. (a)

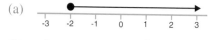

    (b)

    (c)

    (d)

3. $-3, \ -2, \ -1, \ 0, \ 1$

4. $4, \ 5, \ 6$

5. (a) $-1, \ 0, \ 1, \ 2$ (b) $1, \ 2$
    (c) $-1, \ 0, \ 1$

6. (a) $x > 7$ (b) $-2 < x \leqslant 1$

7. $y > -\frac{3}{5}$

8. $1 : \textbf{B}, \quad 2 : \textbf{C}, \quad 3 : \textbf{D}, \quad 4 : \textbf{A}$

9. (a) (b)

    $x + y = 3$
    R
    $y = 1$

10. $x \leqslant 20,$
    $y \geqslant 5,$
    $2y \leqslant x$

11. (a) (b)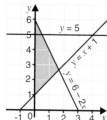

    $y = 5$
    $y = x + 1$
    $y = 6 - 2x$

12. (a) $x < 5$ (b) $x > 2\frac{2}{5}$

13. (a) $-5 \leqslant x < 1$ (b) $n = 0$

14. (a) (i) $x \leqslant 5$ (ii) $x > 2$
    (b) $3, \ 4, \ 5$

SECTION 19

Exercise 19   Page 46

1. (a) $x^2 - 7x$ (b) $x^2 + 3x - 10$
    (c) $x^2 - 2x - 15$ (d) $2x^2 + 5x - 3$

2. (a) $10x + 3$ (b) $6x^2 + 5xy - 4y^2$

3. $9x^2 + 12xy + 4y^2$

4. (a) $x(x - 6)$ (b) $(x + 3)(x + 3) = (x + 3)^2$
    (c) $(x + 5)(x - 3)$ (d) $(x - 1)(x - 3)$

5. (a) $2(x + 4y)$ (b) $3ac(c - 2)$
    (c) $(x - 3)(x - 6)$

6. $(x - 3)(x + 3)$

7. (a) $a + 4$ (b) $x - 3$ (c) $\frac{x}{5}$ (d) $\frac{x}{2}$

8. (a) $x = 0$ or $x = -5$
    (b) $x = 3$ or $x = -2$
    (c) $x = -1.5$ or $x = 1$

9. (a) $2x^2 + x - 15$
    (b) (i) $(x - 1)(x + 7)$
       (ii) $x = 1$ or $x = -7$

10. (a) $5x(x - 2)$ (b) $x = 0$ or $x = 2$

11. (a) $x = 0$ or $x = 3$
    (b) $x = 1$ or $x = 2$
    (c) $x = -2$ or $x = 3$

12. $x = -1$ or $x = 5$ **13.** $x = 4$ or $x = 7$

14. (a) $(2x + 1)(x - 3)$
    (b) $x = -0.5$ or $x = 3$

15. $x = -1$ or $x = 0.5$

16. $1 : \textbf{B}, \quad 2 : \textbf{C}, \quad 3 : \textbf{D}, \quad 4 : \textbf{A}$

17. (a)

x	-3	-2	-1	0	1	2	3
y	18	8	2	0	2	8	18

    (b)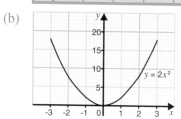

    $y = 2x^2$

    (c) (i) $y = 12.5$
       (ii) $x = 2.45$ or $x = -2.45$

18. (a)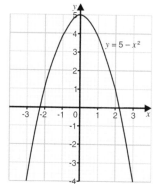

    $y = 5 - x^2$

    (b) 5   (c) $x = 2.2$ or $x = -2.2$

19. (a)

x	-2	-1	0	1	2	3
y	16	7	2	1	4	11

(b)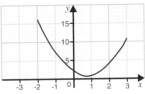

(c) The graph does not cross the line $y = 0$.

(d) 0.9, correct to 1 d.p.

20. (a) Table of values to draw graph.

-3	-24
-2	-6
-1	0
$-\frac{1}{2}$	0.375
0	0
$\frac{1}{2}$	-0.375
1	0
2	6
3	24

(b) $x = 2.3$, correct to 1 d.p.

(c) $x = 0$, $x = -1$ or $x = 1$

21.

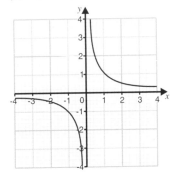

22. (a) $(3 + x)(3 + x) = 9 + 6x + x^2$

(b) $9 + 6x + x^2 = 10$
$$x^2 + 6x = 1$$

23. $x = 3.9$

Section Review   Page 48

1. (a) $5x$ (b) $3a - 4b$ (c) $3m^2$

2. (a) 15   (b) $\frac{1}{2}$ (c) -1

3. (b) $(-1, 1)$

4. (a) $5t$ pence   (b) $t + 5$ pence

5. (a) $x = 10$ (b) $x = 2$ (c) $x = 3$

6. 10

7. (a) 30

(b) 50th term is an odd number.
All even terms are odd numbers.

8. (a) (i) $3x$ (ii) $3a + 2b$ (iii) $3a + 6$

(b) $8x + 1$

9. (a) 7   (b) 1

10. (a) 31, 43

(b) Add the next even number to the last term.

11. (a)

x		-1	0	1	2	3
$y = 3x - 2$		-5	-2	1	4	7

(c) $(0, -2)$

12. (a) $x = -3$ (b) $x = 2.5$ (c) $x = 3$

13. $C = 27n$ **14.** 7

15. (a) $x - 3$ years

(b) $4x$ years

(c) $x + (x - 3) + 4x = 45$
$$x = 8$$
Louisa 5 years,   Hannah 8 years, Mother 32 years

16. (a) (i) $a = 3.5$ (ii) $t = -1$

(b) $x + x - 3 + x + 7 = 25$
$$3x + 4 = 25$$
$$x = 7$$

17. (a) $p = 5$ (b) $q = -\frac{1}{2}$ (c) $y = \frac{1}{4}$

18. $P = bh + c$

19. (a) 11 pounds   (b) $L = \frac{22K}{10}$

(c) $K = 25$

20. (a) (i) $3(a - 2)$ (ii) $k(k - 2)$

(b) (i) $5x + 15$ (ii) $m^2 - 4m$

(c) (i) $x = -1$ (ii) $x = \frac{1}{2}$

21. (a)

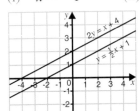

(b) Lines are parallel, same gradient.

22. $x = 15$ **23.** (a) -5 (b) $2x - 3$

24. (a)

x	-2	-1	0	1	2	3
y	1	-2	-3	-2	1	6

(b)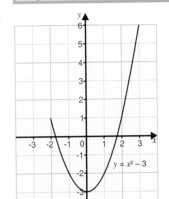

(c) $x = -1.7$ or $x = 1.7$, correct to 1 d.p.

25. (a) 21, 25
(b) Add 4 to the last number.
(c) $4n - 3$

26. $x = 3.25$

27. (a) Missing entries: 20, 27
(b) (i) 65
(ii) 10 + 10th triangular number (55) = 65
(c) $n + \dfrac{n(n + 1)}{2}$
(d) 5049

28. (a) $x < 1\frac{1}{2}$ (b) $-1,\ 0,\ 1$

29. A: **Q**, B: **S**, C: **R**, D: **P**

30. 104 cm³

31. $x = \dfrac{y + 5}{2}$

32. (a) A: $x = 2$, B: $y = 1$, C: $x + y = 2$
(b) $x \leqslant 2,\ y \leqslant 1,\ x + y \geqslant 2$

33. (a)

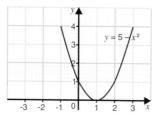

(b) $x = 1$
(c) $x = -0.4$ or $x = 2.4$

34. (a) 20
(b) (i) $(x - 2)(x - 3)$
(ii) $x = 2$ or $x = 3$

35. (a) (i) $2t(s - 2)$ (ii) $3y(y + 2)$
(iii) $(d - 6)(d + 4)$
(b) (i) $x = 0$ or $x = -2$
(ii) $y = 1$ or $y = 2$
(c) $2x^2 + x - 6$

36. (a) $t = \dfrac{u - v}{f}$ (b) $t = \dfrac{8}{f}$
(c) 1, 2, 4, 5, 8

37. (a)

(b) $x = 1.5,\ y = 1$
(c) $3y = -2x + 7$

38. (a) $x^2 + 4x$ (b) $x = 3,\ y = \frac{1}{4}$

39. (a) (i) p^4 (ii) q^4 (iii) x^6
(b) $3xy(3x - 2y^2)$

40. $y = \dfrac{k}{x}$ and $k = 12$

41. (a) $y = \frac{2}{3}x + 2$ (b) $\frac{3}{4}$

42. (a) $\frac{x}{3}$ (b) $3(x + 2)(x - 2)$
(c) $x = -5$ or $x = 2$

43. $(2x - 1)(x + 1) = 104$
$2x^2 + x - 1 = 104$
$2x^2 + x - 105 = 0$

Exercise 20   Page 53

1. (a) $a = 143°$ (b) $b = 135°$
(c) $c = 48°,\ d = 44°$

2. (a) (i) $p = 55°$
(ii) Vertically opposite angles.
(b) (i) $q = 125°$
(ii) p and q are supplementary angles.

3. (a) $\angle PQR = 47°$ (alternate angles)
(b) $\angle RQS = 68°$

4. (a) $a = 117°,\ b = 117°$
(b) $c = 42°,\ d = 76°,\ e = 62°$
(c) $f = 51°$

5. 110°

6. (a) (i) 124°   (ii) 304°   (b) 6.25 km

7. (b) (i) 250°   (ii) 1530 m

Exercise 21   Page 54

1. (a) $a = 97°$ (b) $b = 125°$ (c) $c = 43°$

2. (a) $e = 42°$ (b) $f = 69°$

3. $x = 130°$ ΔPQR is isosceles, $\angle PQR = \angle PRQ$

4. (a) (i) $x = 75°$
(ii) Corres. $\angle$'s, $\angle BDE$
(b) (i) $y = 50°$
(ii) $55° + 75° + y° = 180°$

5. (a) $x = 64°$ (b) $y = 122°$

7. (a) 9 cm²   (b) 10 cm²   (c) 13.5 cm²

8. (b) 15.2 cm²   **9.** 14 cm²

10. $YP = 4.8$ cm

Exercise 22   Page 57

1.

2. (a) **A**, **E**
(b) **N**
(c) **O**

3. (a) (i) 2 (ii) 2   (b) (i) 0 (ii) 1
(c) (i) 2 (ii) 2   (d) (i) 1 (ii) 1
(e) (i) 3 (ii) 3

4.

5.

6. **A** and **F**   **7.** **B** and **D** (SAS)

SECTION 23

Exercise 23 — Page 59

1. (a) Square, rhombus   (b) Trapezium
   (c) Parallelogram, rhombus
2. (a) $a = 70°$ (b) $b = 132°$
   (c) $c = 100°$ (d) $d = 120°$
3. (a) (i) $x = 78°$
      (ii) Supplementary angles
   (b) (i) $y = 130°$
      (ii) Sum of angles in a quad $= 360°$
4. (a) Kite   (b) $\angle ABC = 114°$
6. (a) $1600\,m^2$ (b) $600\,m^2$
7. (a) $30\,cm$ (b) $55.04\,cm^2$
8. (a) $x = 67°$ (b) $52.5\,cm^2$
9. $7\,m$

SECTION 24

Exercise 24 — Page 60

1. (a) $a = 53°$ (b) $b = 115°$ (c) $c = 140°$
2. (a) $a = 60°$, $b = 120°$
   (b) $c = 72°$, $d = 108°$ (c) $e = 67.5°$
3. (a) Equilateral
   (b) (i) $x = 60°$
      (ii) $y = 120°$
   (c) (i) Rhombus   (ii)

4. (a) The shapes cover a surface
      without overlapping and
      leaving no gaps.   (b)

5. (a) $\angle ABC = 144°$ (b) $\angle XCY = 108°$
6. (a) 20 sides   (b) 30 sides
7. (a) $140°$
   (b) Number of sides $= \frac{360°}{20°} = 18$
      Sum of angles $= (18 - 2) \times 180°$
      $ = 16 \times 180°$
      $ = 2880°$
8. $\angle PQX = 151°$
9. Number of sides $= \frac{360°}{30°} = 12$
   Sum of interior angles $= 1800°$

SECTION 25

Exercise 25 — Page 63

1. (a) $a = 65°$ (angle in semi-circle $= 90°$)
   (b) $b = 48°$ (angles in same segment equal)
   (c) $c = 110°$ (angle at centre $= 2 \times$ angle
         at circumference)
   (d) $d = 70°$ (opposite angles of a cyclic
         quad add to $180°$)

128

2. $a = 32°$, $d = 48°$
4. $\angle BCO = 31°$
3. $x = 37°$
5. $y = 70°$
6. $a = 100°$, $b = 40°$, $c = 50°$
7. (a) $\angle ADB = 53°$ (b) $\angle ACD = 32°$
   (c) $\angle ADC = 95°$ (d) $\angle BAD = 95°$
8. $\angle ABC = (x + 90)°$

SECTION 26

Exercise 26 — Page 65

1. (a) $63\,m$ (or $60\,m$)
   (b) $314\,m^2$ (or $300\,m^2$)
2. (a) $46\,m$ (b) $84\,m^2$
3. $81.7\,m^2$
4. $754\,cm^2$
5. $1050\,cm^2$
6. $2.58\,m^2$
7. 106
8. (a) $6360\,cm^2$
   (b) $35.0\,cm$
9. $16\pi\,cm^2$
10. $35.4\,cm$
11. Yes.   Semi-circle $= \frac{1}{2}(\pi \times 10^2) = 50\pi\,cm^2$
    Circle $= \pi \times 5^2 = 25\pi\,cm^2$

SECTION 27

Exercise 27 — Page 67

1.

2. (a)
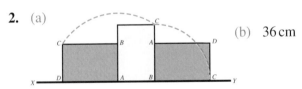
     (b) $36\,cm$

3. (a)

(representative; main diagram)
   (b) $8.4\,km$

4. (a) (b)
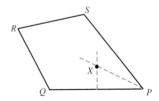
   (c) $PX = 3.9\,cm$

Page 69

1. (a)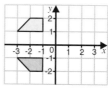

(b)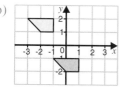

(c)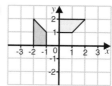

2. (a) Rotation, 90° anticlockwise, about (0, 0).

(b) Translation with vector $\begin{pmatrix} 4 \\ -3 \end{pmatrix}$.

(c) Enlargement, scale factor 3, centre (0, 0).

3. (a) (i) $x = -1$ (ii) $\begin{pmatrix} -1 \\ 2 \end{pmatrix}$

(iii) Centre (0, 2), scale factor 2.

(b)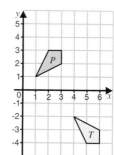

5. (a) Reflection in line $x = 0$ (y axis).
(b) Rotation, 90° clockwise, about (0, 0).

6. Enlargement, scale factor $\frac{1}{3}$, centre (2, 5).

7. (a)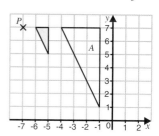

(b) Reflection in line $y = x$.

8. (a) Translation with vector $\begin{pmatrix} 3 \\ 2 \end{pmatrix}$.

(b)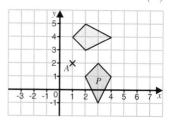

Page 72

1. (a) **C.**
$\mathbf{A} = 24\,cm^3$, $\mathbf{B} = 24\,cm^3$, $\mathbf{C} = 27\,cm^3$

(b) (i) 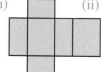 (ii) $52\,cm^2$

(c) **B**: $56\,cm^2$

2. R

3. (a) $24\,m^3$ (b) $68\,m^2$

4. $1530\,cm^3$

5. (a) $414\,cm^2$ (b) $405\,cm^3$

6. $AB = 3.5\,cm$

7. (a) 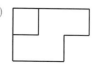 (b)

8. $26.7\,cm^3$

9. (a) $36.9\,m^2$ (b) $32\,cm$

10. (a) $32\,673\,cm^2$ (b) $10\,cm$

Page 74

1. (a) $XY = 10\,cm$ (b) $AC = 1.2\,cm$

2. (a) Ratio of widths $= 1 : 2$ **but** ratio of lengths $= 5 : 7$.
(b) $7.5\,cm$

3. (a) $PQ = 3.75\,cm$ (b) $AC = 5.2\,cm$

4. 19.6 inches

5. (a) $CD = 12\,cm$ (b) $BC = 10\,cm$

6. (a) $\angle ABE = \angle ACD$ (corres. $\angle$'s)
$\angle AEB = \angle ADC$ (corres. $\angle$'s)
$\angle EAB = \angle DAC$ (angle A common)
(b) (i) $AC = 4.8\,cm$ (ii) $AE = 2.8\,cm$

7. (a) $\angle ABC = \angle CDE$ (alt. $\angle$'s)
$\angle BAC = \angle CED$ (alt. $\angle$'s)
$\angle ACB = \angle DCE$ (vert. opp. $\angle$'s)
(b) $DE = 4\,cm$

Page 76

1. $BC = 13\,cm$ **4.** 8.94 units

2. $PQ = 8\,m$ **5.** $RS = \sqrt{48}\,cm$

3. $28.7\,cm$ (or $4\sqrt{3}\,cm$)

6. $AD = 17.7$ cm

7. (a) 13 cm²

   (b) $AB = 5.4$ cm

8. 45.6 cm

9. 5.7 cm

SECTION 32

Exercise 32   Page 78

1. $x = 4.2$ cm

2. (a) $AB = 6.38$ cm   (b) $AB = 5.63$ cm

3. (a) 2.63 m   (b) 66.4°

4. $TE = 13.4$ m   **5.** 286°   **6.** 138 m

SECTION 33

Exercise 33   Page 81

1. (a) 6 km   (b) 60 g   (c) 60 cm²   (d) 60 m³

2. 36.25 km   **3.** 8 pounds   **4.** 15

5. 1 kg pot.   1 kg pot: $\frac{1000}{150} = 6.6\ldots$ g/p

             1 lb pot: $\frac{1 \times 1000}{2.2 \times 71} = 6.4\ldots$ g/p

6. Debbie is taller.   5 ft 4 in = 160 cm

   Joyce is heavier.   9 st 2 lb = 58.2 kg

7. £878   **9.** (a) $d = 91.5$ km

8. 165 mm   (b) 91.5 km $\leqslant d < 92.5$ km

10. The scales are only accurate to the nearest 100 g, so weights can only be given correct to 1 d.p.

11. (a) 57 cm   (b) 63 cm

12. (a) πr^2 and $2bh$ (b) πr^3 and $b^2 h$

Section Review   Page 82

1. (a) $a = 67°$ Angles in a triangle add to 180°.

   (b) $b = 54°$ Isosceles Δ.

           $b = 180° - (2 \times 63°)$.

   (c) $c = 126°$ Angles in a quadrilateral add to 360°.

           $c = 180° - (360° - 306°)$

2. (b) Square, rectangle   (c) Square

3. (a) E.g.   (b) E.g.

4. (a) E.g.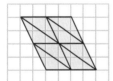

   (b) No.

   Only equilateral triangles, squares and hexagons tessellate.

   Interior angle must divide into 360° a whole number of times.

5. (a) (i)   (ii) 46 cm²

     (b) 2.5 cm

6. $\angle PQR = 120°$

7. **B** and **E**   (ASA)

8. Height 175 cm,   weight 70 kg.

9. (a) Reflection in the line $x = 5$.

   (b) Rotation, 90° anticlockwise, about (0, 0).

   (c) (i)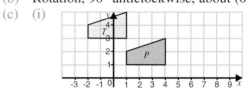

     (ii) 3 units to the right and 2 units down.

10. (a) $a = 40°, b = 95°, c = 135°$ (b) $d = 40°$

11. (a) (i) 5 cm   (ii) 100 km

    (b) (i) 060°   (ii) 240°

    (e) (i) 70.5 km   (ii) 69.5 km

12. 30 cm²   **15.**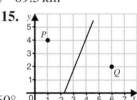

13. (a) 4   (b) 1

14. 297 m²

16. (a) Ext. $\angle = \frac{360°}{6} = 60°$.

       $a =$ int. $\angle = 180° - 60° = 120°$

    (b) $b = 15°$

17. (a) 2.6 m²   (b) 3.9 m³   (c) 17 420 kg

18. Footpaths HX, XS shorter by 171 m.

    Footpaths 850 m,   Waverly Crescent 1021 m.

19.

20. (a) 28.3 km

    (b) 298°

21. 14π cm

22. (a) (b)

   (c) Enlargement, scale factor $\frac{1}{2}$, centre $(-7, 6)$.

23. (a) abc has dimension 3 (volume)

    (b) πa **and** $\sqrt{a^2 - c^2}$ **and** $2(a + b + c)$

24. (a) 125 cm   (b) 40 cm

    (c) 140°   (d) 118.5 cm

25. (a) $BE = 4$ cm   (b) $DE = 12$ cm

26. (a) $a = 35°$ (angles in same segment)

       $b = 145°$ (opp. angle of cyclic quad)

    (b) $c = 61°$ (angle in a semi-circle = 90°)

    (c) $x = 60°$ (tangent meets radius at 90°)

27. (a) $OY = 63$ cm   (b) $\angle XOY = 16.7°$

Exercise 34 — Page 86

1. (a)

Time (t minutes)	Tally	Frequency
$0 \leq t < 30$	‖‖‖	5
$30 \leq t < 60$	‖‖‖ ‖‖‖ ‖‖	12
$60 \leq t < 90$	‖‖‖ ‖‖	7
$90 \leq t < 120$	‖‖‖	5
$120 \leq t < 150$	‖	1

(b) $30 \leq t < 60$
(c) More homework may be set on a Wednesday night. Some homework may be done more quickly.

2. E.g.

Year	M/F	Breakfast today	2 years ago
10	M	Cereal, toast	less
11	F	Grapefruit, yogurt	more
11	F	Toast	same
11	M	Boiled egg, toast	same

3. (a) (i) Too personal.
(ii) In which age group are you?
Under 16 ☐ 16 to 19 ☐ Over 19 ☐
(b) (i) Only students already using the library are sampled.
(ii) Give to students as they enter (or leave) the college.

4. Please give the reason why you no longer attend the Youth Centre.

Unsuitable opening hours ☐
Attend new sports centre ☐
Bullying ☐

Other (please state) . . . .

5. (a)

	Theatre	Art gallery	Science museum	Totals
Girls	11	9	7	27
Boys	8	2	13	23
Totals	19	11	20	50

(b) 7

6. E.g. Two thirds of men were over 45.
All women are aged 16 to 45.
Twice as many women as men.

7. No. Men: $\frac{180}{200} = 90\%$ Women: $\frac{240}{300} = 80\%$
Higher proportion of men can drive.

Exercise 35 — Page 89

1. (a) Each team played 25 matches.
(b) Range: 2, mode: 2
(c) Women's team had a larger range (5) and higher mode (3).

2. (a) 12
(b) 22°C
(c) 14°C
(d) 15°C

3.

Flavour	Angle
Strawberry	128°
Orange	40°
Peach	72°
Blackberry	32°
Other	88°

4. (a) £600
(b) £200

5. (a) 60%
(b) 7 : 11
(c)

Injury	Fatal	Serious	Minor	None
Angle	16°	28°	100°	216°

6. (a)

Boys		Girls	2|5 means 2.5 cm
	2	5	
5 5	3	0 5 5 5	
5 5 5 5 0 0	4	0 5 5	
0 0	5	0 5	

(b) Girls have a larger range (3.0 cm) than boys (1.5 cm).

7. (a) 108° (b) £15 750

Exercise 36 — Page 92

1. (a) £9
(b) £10.50
(c) £11.50
(d) Median.
Mode is the lowest price and mean is affected by the one higher-priced meal.

2. 38

3. (a) 29 (b) 9 (c) 6
(d) 8 (e) 6

4. (a) 11 to 15 (b) 16.4

5. 29 minutes

Exercise 37 — Page 94

1. (b) 8°C
(c) (i) 16°C
(ii) Actual temperatures are only known at times when readings are taken.

2. (a)

Weight (*w* grams)	Tally	Frequency
$490 \leqslant w < 495$	||	2
$495 \leqslant w < 500$	̶H̶H̶T̶ ̶H̶H̶T̶ |	11
$500 \leqslant w < 505$	̶H̶H̶T̶ |	6
$505 \leqslant w < 510$	̶H̶H̶T̶ |||	8
$510 \leqslant w < 515$	|||	3

(c) $495 \leqslant w < 500$

3. (b) $10 \leqslant d < 15$

4. Vertical scale is not uniform.
Balls do not match scale.

5. (a) $80 \leqslant age < 90$ (b)   40
(c)   (ii)   Women:

Age (*a* years)	Frequency
$60 \leqslant a < 70$	1
$70 \leqslant a < 80$	5
$80 \leqslant a < 90$	13
$90 \leqslant a < 100$	6

(iii)   More men under 80 than women.
Only women aged over 90.
Women have greater range of ages.

6. (a)   7   (b)   3   (c)   67

7. 18

8. (a)   (c)

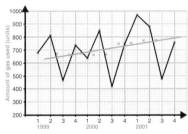

(b)   675,   665,   675,   662.5,   665,   747.5,
755,   772.5,   775
(d)   Slight increase in units used.

SECTION **38**

Exercise **38**   **Page 96**

1. (a)   (i)   *C*   (ii)   *A*   (iii)   *B*   (b)   *C*
2. (b)   Negative correlation.
As engine size increases,
fuel economy decreases.
(d)   Points are close to the line of best fit.
3. (a)   36   (b)   60   (c)   No
(d)   Yes   (e)   Positive
4. (b)   Negative correlation.
As engine size increases, the time taken
to travel 500 m decreases.
(d)   16 seconds

5. (b)   Negative correlation.
As temperature increases, the time taken
for a 2 cm ice cube to melt decreases.
(d)   50 minutes
(e)   24.5°C
(f)   At 35°C the line of best fit gives a time
less than zero, which is impossible.

SECTION **39**

Exercise **39**   **Page 99**

1. (a)   (i)   66 m   (ii)   16 m
(b)

2. (a)   (i)   10 kg   (ii)   7 kg
(b)

3. (a)   £450   (b)   £100
(c)   The average price paid for a computer is
much higher than for a television.
Computers have a smaller variation in
price than televisions.
4. (a)   260 g
(b)   Cooking apples
(c)   180 g
(d)   The average weight of cooking apples is
larger and they have a greater variation
in weight than eating apples.
5. (a)   70   (c)   18 seconds   (d)   24%

SECTION **40**

Exercise **40**   **Page 102**

1. (a)

Second spinner

	2	3	4	5
1	1	2	3	4
1	1	2	3	4
2	0	1	2	3
3	1	0	1	2

First spinner

(b)   1
(c) $\frac{5}{16}$

2. (a) $\frac{2}{5}$ (b)   0.6
3. (a) $\frac{9}{20} = 0.45$
(b)   2,   3,   3,   4,   5.
Numbers 2, 3, 4, 5 have occurred and
3 has occurred twice as often as other
numbers.
(c)   100.   Relative frequency of 5 is $\frac{1}{5}$.
$\frac{1}{5} \times 500 = 100$

4. (a) HHH, HHT, HTH, HTT,
      THH, THT, TTH, TTT

    (b) $\frac{3}{8}$

5. (a) $\frac{5}{8}$ (b) $\frac{7}{8}$

6. (a)

    (b) 0.28   (c) 0.54

7. (a) 0.7   (b) 0.4

    (c) Probability of passing = 0.7
       Probability of failing = 0.3
       0.7 > 0.3

    (d) 700   (e) 0.42   (f) 0.18

Section Review   Page 104

1. (a) (i) 30   (ii) 60

    (b) $110 \leqslant h < 120$

2. (a) (i)

Pantomime	Angle
Aladdin	135°
Cinderella	105°
Jack and the Bean Stalk	75°
Peter Pan	45°

    (ii) Aladdin

    (b) (i) 72

       (ii) No.
          Cinderella $= \frac{120°}{360°} \times 100 = 33\frac{1}{3}\%$

3. (a)

×	1	2	3	4
1	1	2	3	4
2	2	4	6	8
3	3	6	9	12

    (b) $\frac{2}{12} = \frac{1}{6}$

    (c) $\frac{4}{12} = \frac{1}{3}$

4. (a) A: Tuff hatchback
       B: Ace supermini
       C: Nippy sports
       D: Mega estate

5. (a) $\frac{5}{12}$ (b) $\frac{2}{3}$ (c) $\frac{3}{4}$

6. 7.6

7. Ask what foods they ate **today** in the school canteen. Give choices to tick.

8. (a) 6   (b) 3.55   (c) 3.5

9. 0.7

10. (a)

                           4 | 5 means 4.5 cm

4	5 8 8
5	0 0 4 4 5 8
6	0 2 4 5 5 5 6 8
7	0 2 4

    (b) 2.9 cm   (c) 6.1 cm

11. (a) $\frac{17}{75}$

    (b) Yes. Female: $\frac{12}{50} = 24\%$, Male: $\frac{5}{25} = 20\%$

12. (b) Positive correlation.
       Taller men tend to have a better
       best jump than shorter men.

    (d) (i) 1.68 m   (ii) 5.7 m

13. (b) 65 g   (c) $60 \leqslant w < 80$

14. Many people have milk delivered.
Only one data collection point.
Milk may be for one day or many days.
Milk may be for more than one person.

15. (a) 96%   (b) $\frac{1}{33}$

16. £75, £93   **17.** 304

18. (a)

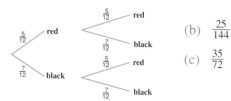

    (b) $\frac{25}{144}$

    (c) $\frac{35}{72}$

19. (a) (ii) Median = 28 minutes,
            Interquartile range = 11 minutes

    (b) Median = 45 minutes,
       Interquartile range = 8 minutes

    (c) Boys' times had a lower average but
       more variation than girls'.

20. (a) 0.49   (b) 0.42

Non-calculator Paper   Page 108

1. 3404

2. (a) 3 is a factor of 15 and 27.   (b) 27

    (c) (i) 15 and 27 (more than 2 factors).

       (ii) 35

3. (a) 10 degrees   (b) −3°C

4. (a) $\frac{1}{2}$ (b) $\frac{7}{20}$

5. 1.05 pm

6. (a) (i) $a = 145°$
       (ii) Supp. ∠'s, $a + 135° = 180°$.

    (b) (i) $b = 83°$
       (ii) Angles in triangle sum to 180°.

    (c) (i) $c = 35°$
       (ii) Vertically opposite angles.

7. (a) (i) 3.28   (ii) 5.4

    (b) 31   (c) −6

8. 2.8 pence

9. (a) (i) $3a - 2$ (ii) $6a^2$ (iii) $2a + 3b$

    (b) (i) $x = -2$ (ii) $x = 4$ (iii) $x = 2.5$

10. (a) 220 cm²   (b) 300 cm³

11.

> 3 cloves of garlic
> 6 ounces of chick peas
> 6 tablespoons of olive oil
> 7.5 fluid ounces of Tahina paste

12. (a) $\angle BAC = 38°$
(b) **P** and **R** (SSS or RHS)
(c) 3 lines of symmetry and rotational symmetry order 3.

13. $\frac{3}{8}$

14. (a) X 1, X 3, Y 1, Y 3
(b) Numbers 1 and 3 are not equally likely.

15. (b) 1560 cm²   **16.** $(-1, 1)$

17. (a)

x	-3	0	3
y	7	1	-5

(b)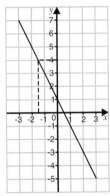
(c) $y = 4$

18. (a) 18 cm   (b) 12 cm²

19. (a) 25%   (b) 90

20. (a) 22 pounds   (b) £2.07

21. (a) (i) 0.2   (ii) 0   (iii) 0.75
(b) 40

22. (a) 26   (b) 85%   (c) 20

23. (a) $\frac{4}{5}$ (b) $1\frac{11}{12}$

24. (a) $x = 2$ (b) $y = 9$

25. $a = 75°$, $c = 75°$

26. (a) $x + (2x - 1) + 3x = 41$
(b) $x = 7$ Numbers on cards: 7, 13, 21

27. 2.5 cm

28. (a) 2 : 3   (b) 12π m

29. Greatest: 11.5 kg, least: 10.5 kg

30. (a) 13   (b) 6 - 10   (c) 30

31. $w = 2b + 2$ **32.**
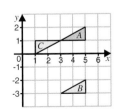

33. $3n - 4$

34. (a) (b)
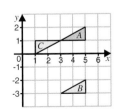
(c) Rotation, 180°, about $(3, -1)$.

35. 10

36. (a) $-2, -1, 0, 1$
(b) (i)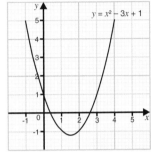
(ii) $9.65 \leqslant t < 9.75$

37. (a) $2^4 \times 3$ (b) $2^2 \times 3^3$ (c) 432

38. (a)

x	-1	0	1	2	3	4
y	5	1	-1	-1	1	5

(b)
$y = x^2 - 3x + 1$

(c) $y = -1.25$ (d) $x = 0.4$ or $x = 2.6$

39. (a) $\cos BAC = \frac{2}{3}$ (b) $BC = \sqrt{5}$ cm

40. (a) 50   (b) $V = 3 \times 4 \times 4 \times 8 = 384$ cm³

41. $x = 11$

42. (a) 3×10^{-8} (b) 3×10^{-10} metres

43. $x = 1.5$, $y = -2$

44. (a) $\frac{5}{6}$ (b) $1\frac{1}{2}$

45. (a) $2x^2 + 5x - 3$ (b) $3a^2(2a - 3)$

46. 40

47. (a) Enlargement, scale factor $\frac{1}{2}$, centre $(0, 1)$.
(b) Rotation, 90° anticlockwise, about $(1, -1)$.

48. (a) $a = 36$ (b) $c = \pm\sqrt{\frac{a}{b}}$

49. $CD = 12$ m

50. (a) (i) $n = 3$ (ii) $n = 6$ (b) 1.2×10^3

51. (a) (i) $P(-5, 0)$ (ii) 0.25
(b) $y = -\frac{2}{5}x + 2$

52. (a)
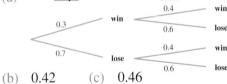
(b) 0.42   (c) 0.46

53. $\sqrt{a^2 + b^2}$ and $4(a + b + c)$.
Both have dimension 1.

54. (a) $(x - 2)(x - 4)$ (b) $x = 2$ or $x = 4$

Calculator Paper   Page 114

1. (a) 684 dollars   (b) £6

2. (a) (i) 1.73   (ii) 0.216
(b) $m = 142.8$

3. (a) $-1, -5$
(b) Subtract 4 from last number.

4. (a) $4m + 5$
(b) (i) $x = \frac{1}{3}$ (ii) $y = 4$
(c) -2

5. (a)

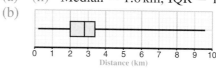

(b) E.g.

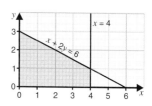

6. (a) -9 (b) 5 (c) $3(x - 2)$

7. £237.60

8. (a) 4.29 (b) 4.27

9. (a) 0.78 (b) 0.3, $\frac{8}{25}$, 33%, $\frac{1}{3}$

10. (a) 0.7 (b) 0.44

11. $24.1\,\text{kg}$

12.

Soup	Angle
Chicken	$120°$
Mushroom	$60°$
Tomato	$75°$
Vegetable	$105°$

13. $58.8\,\text{kg}$

14. $a = 62°$, $b = 60°$, $c = 135°$

15. (a) 15 (b) $28\,\text{g}$ (c) $30\,\text{g}$ (d) $29.3\,\text{g}$

16. Small
Small: $\frac{180}{36} = 5\,\text{g/p}$ Large: $\frac{300}{63} = 4.76\,\text{g/p}$

17. (a) $56.5\,\text{cm}$ (b) $201\,\text{cm}^2$

18. $\frac{1}{15}$

19. (a) $60\,\text{cm}$ (b) $d = \frac{a + b}{3}$

20. (a) 10.94 yards (b) 9.14 metres

21.

23. (a) 0815
(b) (i) Between 0820 and 0835. Steepest gradient.
(ii) $12\,\text{km/h}$

22. 80

24. (b) $2.15\,\text{km}$, $295°$

25. $1260°$

26. (a) $r = 2$ (b) $s = 0.3$ (c) $x = -1.5$

27. (b) Negative correlation.
Countries with higher birth rates tend to have a lower life expectancy.
(c) 52 to 57 (d) 22 to 28

28. $x = 20$

29. (a) $700\,\text{cm}^3$ (b) $13.51\,\text{kg}$

30. (a) 30 (b) $2 \leqslant t < 3$
(c) 2.07 hours

31. $45\,\text{mph}$

32. (a) 0.27
(b) No. High frequency for 1, low frequency for 6.
(c) 1000

33. £14.40

34. (a) £564.66 (b) 15.7625%

35. (a) $AC = 12.4\,\text{m}$ (b) $\angle ABC = 72.1°$

36. $x = 3.8$

37. 61.1%

38. 0.45, correct to 2 s.f. All numbers given to 3 s.f. so answer can only be correct to 2 s.f.

39. (a) $x = 20.6°$ (b) $110.6°$

40. (a) (ii) Median $= 1.6\,\text{km}$, IQR $= 1.1\,\text{km}$
(b)

(c) The average distance for primary pupils is less and they have less variation in the distances travelled.

41. $20\,\text{cm}$

42. (a) $y = \frac{6 - x}{2}$
(b) (i) (ii)

43. (a) (i) $4y^3$ (ii) $12m^5$
(b) $1\frac{1}{8}$ (c) 7.1×10^9

44. (a) $\frac{1}{5}$ (b) $y = -2x + 4$

45. $2p^2q^2(p - 2q)$

46. 8.01×10^{10}

47. (a) $\angle PQR = 53°$
Angle at circumference $= \frac{1}{2} \times$ angle at centre.
(b) $\angle PSR = 127°$
Opposite angles of a cyclic quad supplementary.

48. (a) $\angle ABC = \angle CDE$ (alt. $\angle$'s)
$\angle BAC = \angle CED$ (alt. $\angle$'s)
$\angle ACB = \angle DCE$ (vert. opp. $\angle$'s)
So, ΔABC is similar to ΔEDC.
(b) (i) $\angle ABC = 50°$ (ii) $AB = 4.2\,\text{cm}$

49. (a) -2, -1, 0, 1 (b) $x < \frac{1}{2}$

50. (a) $x = -1$, $y = 1\frac{1}{2}$
(b) (i) $3xy(y + 2)$ (ii) $(m + n)(a - b)$
(c) $2x^2 + x - 6$
(d) $x = 3$ or $x = 4$

51. $\angle BAD = 61.1°$

52. (a) $\frac{1}{16}$ (b) $\frac{1}{6}$ **53.** £63.80

54. (a) $\frac{3}{x - 3}$ (b) $(2x - 4)(x + 3) = 48$
$2x^2 + 2x - 12 = 48$
$2x^2 + 2x - 60 = 0$
$x^2 + x - 30 = 0$

Index ●●●●●●●●●●●●●●●●●●●●●●●●●●●●●●●●●●●